COMPUTE!'s
Quick & Easy Guide to *Microsoft*® *Word* on the IBM PC

William Warren Pitts

COMPUTE!™ Publications,Inc.**abc**
A Capital Cities/ABC, Inc. Company
Greensboro, North Carolina

Copyright 1988, COMPUTE! Publications, Inc. All rights reserved.

Reproduction or translation of any part of this work beyond that permitted by Sections 107 and 108 of the United States Copyright Act without the permission of the copyright owner is unlawful.

Printed in the United States of America

10 9 8 7 6 5 4 3 2 1

ISBN 0-87455-133-1

The author and publisher have made every effort in the preparation of this book to insure the accuracy of the information. However, the information in this book is sold without warranty, either express or implied. Neither the author nor COMPUTE! Publications, Inc. will be liable for any damages caused or alleged to be caused directly, indirectly, incidentally, or consequentially by the information or programs in this book.

The opinions expressed in this book are solely those of the author and are not necessarily those of COMPUTE! Publications, Inc.

COMPUTE! Publications, Inc., Post Office Box 5406, Greensboro, NC 27403, (919) 275-9809, is a Capital Cities/ABC, Inc. company, and is not associated with any manufacturer of personal computers. IBM is a registered trademark of International Business Machines Corporation. Microsoft is as registered trademark of Microsoft Corporation.

To my mother:
She gave me the other half of my perspective.

Contents

Foreword xi

Part One 1

Chapter 1. What Is *Microsoft Word*? 3
   How Is *Microsoft Word* Different from Other Programs?   3
   The Graphics Display 3
   EGA and PGA Display 4
   The User-Friendly Command Interface 4
   Use Either Keyboard or Mouse 5
   The Word Processing Capabilities 6
   Printer Support 6

Chapter 2. New Features and Changes to *Microsoft Word* 4.0 9
   New Features 10
   Changed Features 15
   Enhancements to *Microsoft Word* 17

Chapter 3. Commanding *Microsoft Word* 21
   Keyboard Commands Versus Mouse Commands 21
   Commands Affect Onscreen Formatting 23
   Using the Command Bar 23
   Using the Function Keys 23
   The *Microsoft Word* Command Card 25

Chapter 4. A Quick Start with *Microsoft Word* 4.0 ... 27
   Floppy Drive System 27
   Hard Drive System 27
   Document Files 28
   WYSIWYG 31
   Quitting the Program 32

Chapter 5. Using the Transfer Menu 33
   What Is the Transfer Menu? 33
   Loading a File into Memory 33
   Saving Your Files to Disk 35
   Clearing Text from the Window or Memory 38
   Deleting Files from a Disk 39

Merging Files or Parts of Files into Another 41
Renaming Files 41
Transfer Glossary Commands 42
The Transfer Mode Options 45

Chapter 6. Using the Jump Mode 47
Using the Jump Page Commands 47
Using the Jump Footnote Command 49
Jumping to Beginning or End 50

Part Two 51

Chapter 7. Copying, Deleting, and Inserting Text 53
Cut and Paste 53
Copy, Delete, and Insert 54
Copying Text 56
Deleting Text 59
Using the Delete Command 61
Moving and Inserting Text 62

Chapter 8. An Introduction to Format Commands 65
The Default Settings 66
Changing the Format 66

Chapter 9. Formatting Characters 69
Formatting the Characters 70

Chapter 10. Formatting Paragraphs 77
Formatting Paragraphs 77
Using the Paragraph Format Features 78
Elements of Paragraph Formatting 79
Paragraph Justification 80
Controlling Indention 81
Controlling Spacing 86
Controlling Widows and Orphans 88
Keeping Text Together 89
Speed-Formatting Paragraphs 90
Copying Formatting 92
Printing Columns Side by Side 93

Chapter 11. Page Formatting and Divisions 99
Divisions 99
Changing Page Formats in a Division 99

Controlling the Page Format 100
Division Format Commands and the
   Onscreen Display 101
Controlling Page Size and Margins 101
Formatting for Multiple Columns 103
Using Multiple-Page Formats 106
Printing Page Numbers in Documents 107
The Format Division Layout Menu 109
Printing Line Numbers in Documents 111

Chapter 12. Setting and Using Tabs 115
   Setting Up and Using Tab Stops 116

Chapter 13. Making Tables of Information 123
   Making a Table 123
   Tables Typed in 12-Point, Fixed-Space Fonts 125
   Tables Printed with Different-Sized Fonts 128
   Tables Printed with Proportionally Spaced Fonts ... 130
   Editing and Reorganizing a Table 131

Chapter 14. Using Borders and Lines 139
   Adding Borders with the Format Borders Menu 139
   Drawing Lines with Tabs 146
   Using the Line-Drawing Mode 147

Chapter 15. Printing with *Microsoft Word* 151
   Calling and Using the Print Menu 151
   Normal Printing 151
   Setting the Printing Options 153
   Direct Printing from the Keyboard 162
   Printing a Document to Disk 162
   Printing Glossaries 163
   Printing Form Documents 164
   Queued Printing with *Microsoft Word* 164
   Setting the Pages in a Document 166

Chapter 16. Using Headers and Footers 167
   Using Headers and Footers 167

Chapter 17. Global Searches 175
   Searching for Text 175
   Searching for Formats 179

Chapter 18. Global Search and Replace 183
   Searching and Replacing Text 183
   Searching and Replacing Formats 185

Chapter 19. Using Multiple Text Windows 189
   Opening More Than One Window 189
   Display Modes 190
   How to Use Multiple Windows 192
   Opening New Windows 195
   Closing Windows 199
   Moving Windows 199
   Setting the Window Options 200
   Using the Transfer Options with Windows 202
   Using the Footnote/Endnote Window 205

Chapter 20. Hyphenating Text 209
   Manual Hyphenation 209
   Using Automatic Hyphenation 211

Chapter 21. Numbering Text 213
   Using Different Numbering Systems 216

Chapter 22. Checking Spelling 217
   Running a Spelling Check 218
   Using the Thesaurus 222

Chapter 23. Generating a Table of Contents 223
   Marking the Document for Table of Contents 224
   Generating the Table of Contents 226
   Formatting the Table of Contents 227

Chapter 24. Generating an Index from a Document . 229
   Inserting Index Codes and Entries 230
   Compiling the Index 232
   Formatting the Index for Printing 233

Chapter 25. Using and Making Style Sheets 235
   Understanding Style Sheets 235
   Defining Terms 236
   What Is a Style Sheet? 236
   What Are Style Tags? 237
   For What Are Style Sheets Used? 237

Two Menus That Control Style Sheets 238
Using the Format Style Sheet Menu 239
Using *Microsoft Word*'s Style Sheets 241
Using a Style Sheet 243
Microsoft Word's Standard Style Sheets 245
Using the Gallery Menu 247
Understanding the Gallery Menu 247
Writing and Editing Style Sheets and Style Tags 248

Index 257

Foreword

COMPUTE!'s Quick and Easy Guide to Microsoft Word on the IBM PC shows you the easy road to word processing. In it you'll find an overview of word processing, the *Microsoft Word* package covered in detail, and a reference to the available features. This book grows with you, expanding as your experience and confidence increase. In no time at all, you'll become an old hand at word processing with *Microsoft Word*.

Microsoft Word 4.0 is a triumph, bringing together not only all the necessary tools found in the best word processors but also page description and desktop publishing features. In a way, it's two word processors in one. If you own a video card capable of producing a graphics display, you can set *Microsoft Word* to produce a WYSIWYG (What You See Is What You Get) display to show what the print is going to look like on the page before you actually print it. Or, if you prefer the greater legibility and speed of a text display, you can have that.

COMPUTE!'s Quick and Easy Microsoft Word on the IBM PC is divided into three parts. In it, you'll find an overview of word processing, the *Microsoft Word* package covered in detail, and a reference to the available features. This book grows with you, expanding as your experience and confidence increase. In no time at all, you'll become an old hand at word processing with *Microsoft Word* 4.0.

By the time you've discovered the extent of *Microsoft Word*'s huge array of features, you'll agree that *COMPUTE!'s Quick and Easy Guide to Microsoft Word on the IBM PC* has earned its place beside your computer. Word processing has never been so easy.

Part One

Chapter 1
What Is *Microsoft Word?*

Microsoft Word is the showcase word processing program from Microsoft. It has been on the market for several years now and has earned its popularity by proving itself as a powerful tool for writing of all kinds. The program has gone through numerous changes and revisions and is now available in release 4.0, indicating through its durability that it will continue to grow and change with the needs of the people who use it.

The program works with a graphics interface that conceals the bare-bones technology from its user. It you have a mouse, you can command *Microsoft Word* with the point-and-click method. If you don't have a mouse, you can use the keyboard to call the same menus and move the selector to the option and command of your choice. Every feature is commanded either with a *yes* or *no* or with a multiple-choice response. You are given lists to choose from and common-sense measurements to apply.

How Is *Microsoft Word* Different from Other Programs?

Microsoft Word is different from other programs because of its WYSIWYG (What You See Is What You Get) graphics display, its command/user interface, the number of printers it supports, the way it uses these printers to their full capabilities, and its large array of features.

What makes the most difference is not how each of these work independently, but how they work together. As a joint system, they allow you to work with any kind of document and produce the best printed result possible.

The Graphics Display

The term *WYSIWYG* is a very popular buzzword in the software business today. It means that *Microsoft Word* has a good onscreen representation of the document that will actually be printed. This is also called *onscreen formatting*.

Chapter 1

Onscreen formatting allows you to write your documents and then visually typeset them for printing. This takes the guesswork out of the process. You don't have to embed commands in the text file and hope things work as planned when you print. In most cases, you can see whether something is formatting correctly or not.

EGA and PGA Display *[handwritten: We Don't Have This Anyways]*

Microsoft Word 4.0 has been rewritten to make the best possible use of EGA and PGA graphics. These will produce a video display that is far superior to anything previously available for MS-DOS computers. And *Microsoft Word* can recognize these superior video boards and make use of their capabilities.

The actual quality of the video display depends heavily on the resolution of the monitor you're using and on the capabilities of the video graphics board installed in the computer. Standard monochrome and CGA graphics limit what you see to 23 lines and to 80 columns of text onscreen.

If you have an EGA or PGA graphics system, then what you can do with *Microsoft Word* becomes even more impressive. Those graphics systems will display about twice as much onscreen. Depending on the actual system, that means around 46 lines and 12–130 columns of text onscreen.

What is even more impressive is that the actual *resolution* (the clarity) of what you see is also enhanced. Onscreen formatting moves closer to showing you actual changes in font style and size. *Microsoft Word* can also work with the so-called WYSIWYG monitors now becoming increasingly popular among desktop publishers.

The User-Friendly Command Interface

The term *user-friendly* is another buzzword in the computer business. It means that hardware and software developers are working more and more to let you use complicated technology while hiding the technological bones of what you are using. If you're like most people, you don't care how something works. What you're concerned with is how much it will help you do your work and how easy it is to use.

What is Microsoft Word?

Microsoft Word has word processing features that you can run simply by aiming your mouse pointer and clicking the mouse button. That's all it takes to execute any *Microsoft Word* command or to set up any of its word processing features.

All of *Microsoft Word's* commands and features are available through command menus. You can't (or won't) use every feature on every menu in every document you write. That wouldn't be practical. There are many features that you may never use at all.

First, you must know what kind of document you have to write and what it's supposed to look like. Then, you have to learn how to use the features that make your document print that way. You don't have to worry about the other things on the menus.

Whatever you're doing, formatting your documents is basically a matter of picking the features you need from one menu or another. When you pick a command, turn on a feature, and set up things the way you want, the printer will give you the exact document you need.

Use Either Keyboard or Mouse

To command *Microsoft Word*, you can use either the keyboard or the mouse. Both methods call up the command menus and let you pick out and set up the features and commands. When you use the keyboard, it helps to think of the process as issuing Escape commands, because you press the Esc (Escape) key and then type command letters to get to the menu or to execute the command that you need.

`Esc` If you don't have a mouse installed in your computer system, you should seriously consider one for use with *Microsoft Word*, even if you're using someone else's computer at work. The price of mice has dropped, and there are several on the market for a hundred dollars or less. While you can execute every command and feature through the keyboard, there are some things that are simply faster and easier to do with the mouse.

Chapter 1

You'll find that it's best to use both the keyboard and the mouse. One of the biggest problems in word processing is the monotony of sitting at the keyboard all day long. Prolonged monotony can destroy creativity and productivity. Some things work easier with the mouse than with the keyboard; other things work better when executed through the keyboard. Much of this is personal preference. When you have both systems to use, you can add variety to your day and maybe even have a little fun.

The Word Processing Capabilities

Since its first release, *Microsoft Word* has been known for the large number of features it offers. There is a feature or option to cover virtually every word processing need. You can write, edit, typeset, and print any kind of document.

When you sit down to a word processor to write a document, you have a general idea about what kind of document you want to write. It's going to be a letter, a memo, a sales report, the minutes of the last engineering meeting, a brochure touting a new product, a screenplay or teleplay, a master's thesis or doctoral dissertation, or something else.

You may have a less clear idea about how the actual document will roll out of the printer. *Microsoft Word* makes it easier to prepare your document while it's still in memory.

Printer Support

Microsoft Word supports a wide range of printers and uses them to the limits of their capabilities. *Microsoft Word* has a printer driver for virtually every printer currently on the market. It even has printer drivers for printers no longer being sold but still heavily used in businesses and offices across the country.

Whether you're using a 9- or 26-pin dot-matrix printer, a daisy-wheel printer, an ink-jet printer, or a laser printer, you either will find its driver on the printer list or will be able to customize *Microsoft Word* to meet its specifications.

Microsoft Word has special support for the Hewlett-Packard LaserJet series of printers. It has a separate driver for

What is Microsoft Word?

each of the popular font cartridges sold for that machine. If you are using a LaserJet with the standard B font cartridge, *Microsoft Word* can add italics, boldface, and single- or double-underlining to every font on that cartridge. In addition, *Microsoft Word* has built-in special support for the M cartridge, which Microsoft developed jointly with Hewlett-Packard.

You'll have to study your own professional documents and know their parameters. If you work for a company that has a particular style or way of doing documents, you must learn what that style is. If one kind of document must be done one way and another document another, then learn what the elements of each kind of document are.

If you know what documents you need to write and what they're supposed to be like when they're finished, then *Microsoft Word* and this book can help you write, edit, format, and print them.

7

Chapter 2

New Features and Changes to *Microsoft Word* 4.0

Microsoft Word 4.0 has been substantially rewritten to help you get your work done. These changes include new features as well as enhancements to old ones. Also changed are some of the ways of using the keyboard and for choosing commands and features. Before going through this chapter, it would be a good idea to run *Microsoft Word* so you can see the command line.

You will note a section near the bottom of the screen that contains the text as shown in Figure 2-1.

Figure 2-1. The Command Bar

```
COMMAND: Copy Delete Format Gallery Help Insert Jump Library
         Options Print Quit Replace Search Transfer Undo Window
```

The command bar is known variously as the *command field*, the *command area*, the *edit menu*, or the *main menu*. In this book, the section at the extreme bottom of the screen that contains the editing commands in alphabetical order will be identified as the command bar.

During the course of this book, you'll often see graphic representations of keys in the margin. They will resemble this one:

`Esc` In this case, it means that you press the Esc key to activate the command bar. In other cases, it will illustrate how to perform other functions. When you see Esc in combination with other keys, press the keys in sequence. For instance, if you see Esc and *T*, press Esc and then T. When you see Alt, Ctrl, or Shift in combination with other keys, it means that you should hold down the first key and

9

Chapter 2

press the following keys. If you see Alt-F9, hold down the Alt key while pressing F9.

Press the Esc key to highlight the choices in the command bar. You may use the cursor keys to select the alternatives. When you select one, you'll be taken to a second-level menu. From this menu, you'll select the actual feature you want to use. Begin by highlighting Library. Press Enter. The second menu will include Document-retrieval. That is the first feature to be discussed in the next section.

Sometimes, second-level menus give way to third-level menus, and so on. All of these menus are intended to make *Microsoft Word* as easy to use as possible, but after you have used them for a while, you'll discover that they can be time consuming and that they interrupt the creative flow of writing. By that time, you'll be familiar enough with the program to make use of macros, and you'll know other special ways to enter commands that will streamline your writing. These topics will be covered in detail later in the book.

New Features

Document-retrieval. If you write a large number of text files and store them on a hard drive, you know it can be a major irritation to keep track of them. With electronic documents, it can be difficult to know the exact contents of a file, who wrote it, when it was last worked on, and by whom. See Figure 2-2.

Figure 2-2. Summary Sheet

```
chapter 9.doc♦
```

```
SUMMARY INFORMATION
    title: chapter 9                    version number: 2
    author: William Warren Pitts        creation date: 5/21/88
    operator:                           revision date: 5/30/88
    keywords:
    comments: Document-retrieval is under Library on the command bar
Enter text
Pg1 Li1 Co14     {}                                    OT    Microsoft Word
```

New Features and Changes to Microsoft Word *4.0*

Each document or text file now has a summary sheet attached to it electronically. This summary sheet contains very specific information about the file itself, including the following.

- Title: The title of the text file as it is stored on disk.
- Author: The name of the author of that text file.
- Operator: The name or initials of the person currently running *Microsoft Word* on the computer system. This is useful when you are using a computer that others can access.
- Keywords: These are passwords you can assign to a specific text file in order to keep unauthorized people from accessing a text file and altering its contents.
- Comments: Brief personal comments about a text file that refer specifically to the text file.
- Version Number: A code number you can assign to a text file to indicate what version of a document the text file represents.
- Creation Date: The actual date the text file was first saved to disk. This will remain unchanged however many times the document is revised and saved again to disk storage.
- Revision Date: The date the text file was last saved to disk storage. *Microsoft Word* will retrieve this information from the disk directory and display it when you call up the summary sheet.

This summary sheet information provides an additional layer of security when you are using *Microsoft Word* in an office system that's set up for networking. The summary sheet is very similar to those used in dedicated word processing systems provided by Wang and IBM. Those systems require individual operators to log on before documents can be written or edited, and users may protect their work from unauthorized changes by assigning passwords to the individual text files.

You can use the information in the summary sheet to locate and retrieve the specific documents you need. Or you can use any text in a text file as a key to search for other text files that contain the same text. This provides you with an electronic cross-referencing service that can save you an enormous amount

11

Chapter 2

of time. Once you locate a document through Document-retrieval, you can load it directly into a text window with a DR Load command instead of having to use the Transfer Load command (more about these commands later).

Using Document-retrieval. The Document-retrieval functions are located in the Library features on the command bar. This summary sheet information may be seen by:

- Selecting the Document-retrieval command from the Library selection on the command bar.
- Using the View command to select the method and order of showing the information.

To look at the summary sheet for a file already loaded into memory, select Document-retrieval and then select the Update command from the menu that appears.

Macros. Macros allow you to specifically redefine the keyboard. Macros allow you to record almost any sequence of keystrokes, commands, and edits and then carry them out (or insert them into a text file) by later typing a simple key sequence.

By defining macros, you can assign specific commands—or strings of commands—to designated keystroke sequences. Later, when you use that sequence of keystrokes, you execute the commands assigned to that combination.

This means you can execute complicated commands immediately, instead of going through the layers of command menus to get to those commands. You can define macros by recording actions as you perform them or by typing all the key names, commands, text, and instructions in the order you want to store them in that macro.

Microsoft has already prepared a number of macros for you to use with *Microsoft Word*. These macros are stored on your *Microsoft Word* Utilities disk.

Linking *Microsoft Word* with spreadsheet data. You can now link *Microsoft Word* with data files from three major spreadsheet programs. This means you can draw the data directly from the data file instead of having to type it into the file from the keyboard.

New Features and Changes to Microsoft Word *4.0*

Microsoft Word provides built-in support for accessing and updating this spreadsheet information. If you have data created in *Microsoft Excel* or *Multiplan* and *Lotus 1-2-3* formats, you can retrieve that data with *Microsoft Word* and use it in your text files.

This feature is available under the Library selection on the command bar, under the Link command.

Drawing lines, boxes, and borders. *Microsoft Word* 4.0 lets you draw lines, borders, and boxes directly into your text files. These are graphic insertions that can be used to enhance the appearance of a document or to call special attention to parts of a document. Use horizontal lines in your headers or footers. Make information tables easier to read by putting vertical lines between the columns of information. Special paragraphs, like notes to the reader, tips, or warnings, can be made to stand out from a page by enclosing them within boxes. Or you can put borders on a page with vertical lines. These lines and boxes can be printed either normally, in boldface, or as double lines. These are especially attractive if you're printing documents on a laser printer. They will give your document a professional appearance.

To use the Border command, select Format from the command bar and then select Border. Type the capital letter in the options that you want to use, and press Esc to return to the document. A box will be drawn there (if that's what you selected) in which you may type. The box will expand to contain your text. Once placed in a text file, these graphic insertions become a part of the format of the paragraph.

revision-Marks track changes to a document. *Microsoft Word* 4.0 has a useful editing and rewriting feature called *revision-Marks*. When you turn on this feature, *Microsoft Word* will automatically mark any deletions or insertions as you make them in the file. This allows you to keep track of the changes you make to a document during any write-and-edit session.

Microsoft Word will put deletion marks in the document. When you delete text, *Microsoft Word* will strike through the

13

Chapter 2

text instead of making it disappear. If you have a color monitor, these deletion marks will display as red lines.

Microsoft Word will put insertion marks into the file. When you insert text into a file, *Microsoft Word* will display the text in one of the five optional ways you can select. The standard display is Underlined. It will also show insertions in Normal, Boldface, all Uppercase, or Double-Underlined text. If you have a color monitor, these will display in red.

Revision bars are often used in the margins of technical or legal documents to indicate any passages that have been changed. When an editor or reader sees a revision bar, he or she is alerted to the fact that the text may have been varied from the original or standard. You can set *Microsoft Word* to automatically insert revision bars in the margins when changes are made. You then have the option of putting the revision bars in either margin or alternating from side to side. Choosing the third option will print them in the right margin on odd pages and in the left margin on even pages—the outside margins of each page.

Once you have changed a document, the revision-Marks feature allows you to accept or remove the changes by paragraph, section, or throughout the entire document. This means you can make changes to a document and then easily restore the document to its original form if you decide you don't like the changes.

Line numbers. *Microsoft Word* has always been able to tell you what page and column numbers you were on in the document onscreen. It displayed this information in the status line. But previous versions could not display the line number of the current cursor position. Now, in version 4.0, you can toggle line number display on and off and print those line numbers in the hardcopy, if you want. One type of document that uses this feature is the legal brief.

Once turned on, the line numbering counts the number of lines to the bottom of the page and then starts over again when it crosses a page-break line onscreen.

New Features and Changes to Microsoft Word *4.0*

ESC ⟨PRINT⟩ ⟨REPAGINATE⟩

The text file must be paginated before this option can work fully. But after you do that, you can toggle the line number display by selecting Options from the command bar. About midway down the right column, you'll see line numbers: Yes(No). Change this selection to yes by pressing Y. The parentheses around the No option indicate that this is the option currently in effect.

Using graphics or text mode. You have your choice of doing your word processing in either the graphics mode or *Microsoft Word's* fast-text mode. You can toggle back and forth between them with a few keystrokes. In many ways it's more efficient to type in the text display mode. The text mode uses up less memory, and your computer will be able to process it faster. This means input/output operations (like loading and saving the file, keyboard response, and even updating the screen) and moving around within the file will be quicker. Then, if you need to see what your character formats look like,

you can switch to graphics mode. You can set *Microsoft Word* to start up in either mode. To toggle between graphics and text mode, press Alt-F9 (hold down the Alt key and press F9) or select Options and highlight the line in the first column that shows Graphic(Text) and press G. You will then be in graphics mode, if your computer supports graphics mode.

Changed Features

If you aren't familiar with older versions of *Microsoft Word*, you would be well advised to skip this section. If you have used the program in any of its earlier versions, this section will help you make an adjustment to the newest incarnation, version 4.0.

Improved keyboard. *Microsoft Word* no longer has an Alpha command on the command bar. The Alpha command was at best an awkward redundancy. Now you only have to use the Esc key to switch between the document and the menus.

15

Chapter 2

The arrow keys. One very convenient change is the fact that *Microsoft Word* now lets you move the selector within command menus with the arrow keys on the keyboard. Using older versions without a mouse could be very difficult.

The Ctrl key. When you are in the typing mode, you can use the Ctrl key to enhance the functions of the cursor movement keys. When used with the left- and right-arrow keys, it will make the cursor move much faster, jumping from word to word rather than character to character. When used with the Home and End keys, it will make the cursor jump to the top and bottom of the screen page, respectively.

The Shift key. You can use the Shift key with any cursor key to expand or decrease the cursor highlight. Its function will depend on whether the text is already covered with the highlight. With the down-arrow key, it changes the highlight status down through the text file line by line. With the up-arrow key, it changes the highlight status up through the text file line by line. With the left arrow, it changes the highlight to the left. And with the right arrow, it changes the highlight to the right.

The function keys. Each of the programmable function keys on the keyboard can perform four different functions. Press the function key alone or in combination with the Shift, Alt, or Ctrl keys. The Shift-F1 combination (hold down shift and press F1), and the F9 key work differently in *Microsoft Word* 4.0 from the way they worked in version 3.1. For the most convenient use of these function keys, you'll need the Function Key Template that comes with *Microsoft Word*. If you don't have this template, you can buy a version of it at many bookstores or software dealers.

The F1 key. The F1 key displays lists. Some of the command options will display lists of text files, printer drivers, font sizes and types, and similar types of information. In previous versions, these lists were called up by pressing the right-arrow key. In *Microsoft Word* 4.0, you use the F1 key instead. This is because the arrow keys are now used for selector movement in the command menus.

New Features and Changes to Microsoft Word *4.0*

Indention. In previous versions of *Microsoft Word*, keystroke combinations controlled the indention of lines and paragraphs. These combinations were Alt-N, Alt-M, Alt-T, and Alt-F. Those key combinations now indent to the tab stops you have set for the current paragraph. If you haven't set any special tab stops, then these key combinations use the default tab width defined in the command bar Options.

Choosing commands. You can still choose most of the commands from the menus by typing the first letter of the command. But more commands have been added to the menus. Some of those new commands begin with the same letter as an older command. Therefore, you'll need to look at the menu more carefully before you issue a command. Now the rule is that you must type the capital letter in the command name.

Enhancements to *Microsoft Word*

You'll note many improvements in *Microsoft Word* over previous versions.

Speed. Many *Microsoft Word* features now run faster than they did in previous versions of the program. Some of these features are:

- File loading and saving
- Spelling checks
- Cursor and highlight movement
- Scrolling through the text file
- Deleting text
- Backspacing
- Search-and-Replace
- Repagination

You can now adjust the cursor movement speed with the Options command.

Custom display. With *Microsoft Word*, you have a greater control over your onscreen display than ever before. You can remove the border around the text window if you don't want it. This will make room for two more lines and two more columns of text onscreen. It's easier to change the color display

17

Chapter 2

than with earlier versions, and you can change the colors of the command selection names to make it easier to distinguish them at a glance.

These display customizations are available through the command bar Options.

Page-break identification. Previous versions of *Microsoft Word* used only the symbol >> on the left edge of the screen to indicate a page break. That was easy to miss. In *Microsoft Word* 4.0, instead of that nondescript symbol, you'll see a dotted line drawn across the width of the text window. This will leave no doubt where one page ends and the next begins.

Windows. *Microsoft Word's* windows have long allowed you to load documents into memory until your computer's memory fills up. Having multiple text files in memory meant that you could cut and paste text between files to create and improve other text files. There was a drawback: the more windows you opened, the smaller each successive window could be. Smaller windows can hold less type.

Microsoft Word 4.0 now gives you the ability to zoom in on each window you open. When you zoom in on a window, the text in it will fill your entire screen. The window is displayed full-size. You can view it just as though it were the only file in memory.

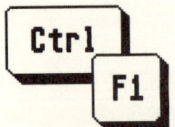

All it takes to zoom in on a text window is to press Ctrl-F1 (hold down the Ctrl key and then press the F1 key). Then you can use the F1 key by itself to move consecutively through each of the windows you have open, zooming in on each of them in turn. This makes it much more convenient to search through the text files for the passages you wish to find. It's easier to mark the text and cut and paste it into the other text file where you need it.

Onscreen command explanations. As an added feature, whenever the highlight is on a command name, *Microsoft Word* will display a brief explanation below the menu. As you move the highlight from name to name, the message displayed will be specific to that command. Each message gives you some useful information about using that command.

New video support. *Microsoft Word* will now work with the following new display hardware: the Hercules GN222; the Genius (in graphics mode); and the IBM VGA mode.

Style sheets. *Microsoft Word* 4.0 allows you to create style sheets by example. Style sheets allow you to format a text file to fit a prearranged form. Using style sheets is far simpler than creating your format each time you write a document. There's also an improvement over style sheets in previous versions of *Microsoft Word*, which required you to define a style sheet by painstakingly setting the parameters for each option to be used in it. Style sheets in version 4.0 allow you to write a document in the proper format and then specify the format from the example you have produced (hence they are style sheets by example).

Spelling checker. The spelling checker functions of *Microsoft Word* have been improved. You don't have to check the spelling of an entire text file at once. Now you can choose to check the spelling of a single word, a paragraph, or a page of your document. The spelling dictionary has been enlarged to 130,000 words.

Thesaurus. Access to the thesaurus has been improved. Now you can use your mouse in the thesaurus window to pick and choose words, replace words with synonyms, move through the synonym list, and do more.

The better a thesaurus works with your word processor, the happier you'll be with it. It can be a powerful tool for improving the quality of your writing. It can help you avoid using the same word over and over again to the point where it begins to lose its communication value in your document.

Outlining. *Microsoft Word's* outlining capability has been improved so you can expand and contract your outline headings to different levels of detail. As a result, you can adjust it to the specific level you need in order to view your progress at a glance, even in a large document.

Table of contents. Once you have created an outline with *Microsoft Word's* outlining feature, there's a quick way to make a table of contents. *Microsoft Word* can use the headings in the outline (providing as many levels as you want) as entries for

Chapter 2

generating a table of contents from that outline. This is quicker and easier than most table of contents generators because it doesn't require that you embed codes in the file.

Merge print. You can test-print a merge printing session without wasting a single sheet of paper or wasting the time it would take your printer to do the job. In order to accomplish this, tell the print merge feature to send the print run to a text file rather than the printer. The merge printing routine will draw the text and/or data from the designated files as normally directed and will create a simulation of the merge printing that would have printed on paper. But this printing run will be handled at electronic speeds, and the only limitation on speed is access times of your mechanical drives. So you don't have to wait, you don't have to use the printer, and you won't use any paper.

Automatic word counting. Whenever you repaginate or print a text file, *Microsoft Word* will automatically count the number of words in the file and display the count in the lower left corner of the screen. At the same time, it also counts and displays the number of lines in the file.

Chapter 3
Commanding *Microsoft Word*

Microsoft Word won't do anything until you tell it to. You will create documents; load old ones into memory; write, edit, and format the text; and then save your changes to storage on disk. When you're ready, you will tell *Microsoft Word* to print out your documents.

Every instruction given to a computer is a command. If you are an old hand at word processing, you will find *Microsoft Word* easy to use. All word processors do the same basic things. You may find old features under different names, and a lot of things will respond to different keypresses. Find the features you want to use, and then learn how to use them.

If you have used an earlier version of *Microsoft Word*, you already know how to use most of its features, so can skip the rest of this chapter. This section will update you on the changes and additions to *Microsoft Word* in the corresponding chapters.

Keyboard Commands Versus Mouse Commands

There are two different ways to execute *Microsoft Word* commands and word processing features. They perform the same functions and differ only in application. This manual calls them *Keyboard Commands* and *Mouse Commands*.

These two methods of entering commands get the same results; the method used is purely a matter of personal choice. Both methods call and use the *Microsoft Word* command menus.

Having the menus means less memorization of commands or referral to the User's Manual. You should be able to quickly grasp and use word processing features that might otherwise confuse you.

Chapter 3

The keyboard control method. All of the *Microsoft Word* features are accessed through the command bar. This bar is called up by pressing the Esc key.

When the command bar is activated, you'll see a list of words that represents all the major commands and functions of the program. These commands are listed in alphabetical order, without consideration of their relative importance. The first command on the bar will be highlighted. To select any command on the bar, just type the first letter of the word of that command. The command bar will be replaced with a menu containing all the commands and features available under that major command.

The command bar, and any of its menus, may be called any time you need them while working on a text file. When a menu is onscreen, its commands may be selected by moving the highlight to the desired function and executed by pressing the Enter key.

No text may be typed into the text file while the menu is activated.

To escape from any menu without making changes, Press the Esc key again. This will send the menu away.

The mouse-driven method. It's easier to use a mouse with *Microsoft Word* than to describe it. You simply "point and click." When the mouse driver is installed, there will be a special mouse pointer onscreen. Just use the mouse to move that cursor to your selection and click a button on the mouse. What could be more simple?

This book strongly recommends using a mouse with *Microsoft Word*. While every *Microsoft Word* command may be issued from the keyboard, it is far easier to use a mouse. You can call the command menus more easily with the mouse, and the mouse cursor may be moved directly to the command selections. *Microsoft Word* was written originally for use in the Macintosh computer, and then it was "ported over" to operate on MS-DOS machines, so nothing could be more natural than interacting with the program through a mouse.

Mixing keyboard and mouse commands. For the best use of all, you will probably discover that some commands or features are easier to execute with the keyboard; others are

Commanding Microsoft Word

easier using the mouse. Much of this will be determined solely by your own personal preferences and by your comfort with the keyboard and mouse.

Commands Affect Onscreen Formatting

Microsoft Word is designed to provide onscreen formatting. Within limits, the document onscreen looks like the document that will be printed. Most features either move you around in the document or control how it looks onscreen. When a feature is used, the results are immediate. Deleted words disappear. Paragraphs automatically format to line spacing and margin settings, and so on, as they are typed. When you rewrite, edit, and use the features, it changes the way the document looks onscreen.

Using the Command Bar

All of *Microsoft Word*'s modes are available through the command bar. This appears at the bottom of the screen whenever you press the Esc key or move the mouse pointer to the bottom of the screen and click the left button. The command bar resembles Figure 3-1.

Figure 3-1. The Command Bar

```
COMMAND: Copy Delete Format Gallery Help Insert Jump Library
         Options Print Quit Replace Search Transfer Undo Window
Edit document or press Esc to use menu
Pg1 Li3 Co32     {}                              OT    Microsoft Word
```

Using the Function Keys

Microsoft Word has been written to use the ten programmable function keys available on the standard PC keyboard. These are normally labeled F1 through F10. Functions assigned to a key may be executed by pressing the key.

   A template of these program key functions comes with *Microsoft Word*. More elaborate versions of these keyboard overlays are available through bookstores and software outlets. Many people find these overlays to be invaluable tools in using *Microsoft Word*.

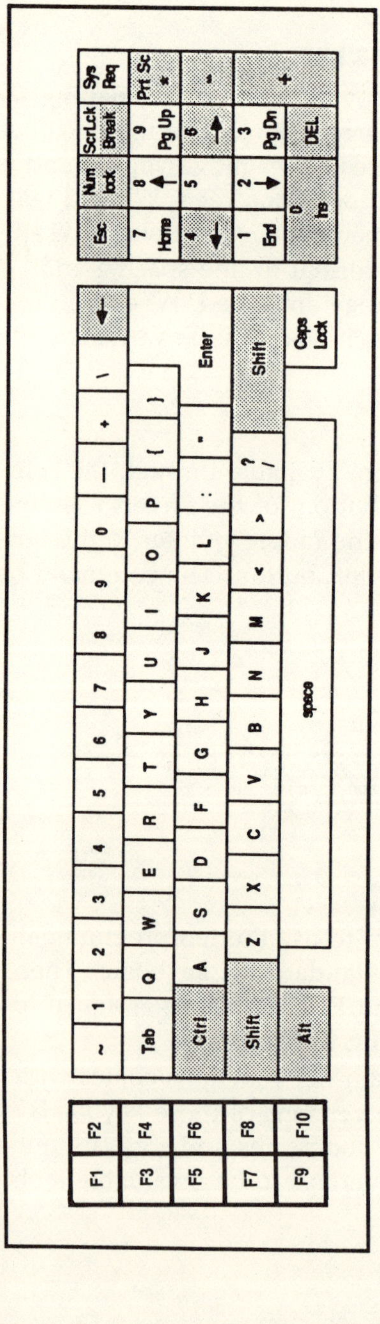

Chapter 3

Figure 3-2. Standard PC Keyboard

The *Microsoft Word* Command Card

Packed with your copy of *Microsoft Word* is a multifold paper card that lists all the features and commands. This is the *Microsoft Word* Command Card. Use it as a quick reference chart and a memory aid. It will save you the time it would take to look up a command in the manual. Once you have familiarized yourself with the capabilities of this system, the card may be all you need to make use of the functions available.

If you don't have a command card, you'll be able to find several good ones through the major bookstore chains and in software supply outlets. These command summaries are invaluable to the first-time user while having to learn how to use *Microsoft Word,* and they are a tremendous help to anyone who uses certain features only occasionally.

Chapter 4
A Quick Start with Microsoft Word 4.0

This chapter was intended to get a first-time user started with *Microsoft Word*.

Floppy Drive System

You must have two drives in order to run *Microsoft Word*. As you use the program, you will have to swap disks in and out of the drives to use the spelling checker and the other utilities.

There are several steps to using *Microsoft Word* with a floppy drive system.

- Boot up your computer in your usual way.
- Put the Program Disk into the A: drive and close the drive door.
- Put the Utility Disk into the B: drive and close the drive door.
- Type *WORD* and then press the Enter key. This is the command to load and run *Microsoft Word*.
- After a moment or two, depending on how fast your drives are, an outlined box will appear onscreen. This is the text window. As you type, all of your text will appear inside this window.
- *Microsoft Word* is loaded and running. It starts up in the write-and-edit mode. You may type and print a new document or load an existing one into memory.

Hard Drive System

If *Microsoft Word* is installed on a hard disk drive, then all of its support files should be on the drive. This means it will be faster and easier to run the program and to access all of its features.

Chapter 4

- Boot the computer and go to the *Microsoft Word* directory. (To learn how to change directories, refer to your MS-DOS user's manual.)
- Type WORD and then press the Enter key. This is the command to load and run *Microsoft Word*.
- After a moment or two, depending on how fast your drive is, an outlined box will appear onscreen. This is the text window. All of your text will appear inside this window as you type.
- *Microsoft Word* is loaded and running. It starts in the write-and-edit mode. You may type and print a new document or load an existing one into memory.

Document Files

When *Microsoft Word* loads and runs, it's instantly in the write-and-edit mode. All you have to do to create any plain document (a letter, a contract, a book, or whatever) is to start typing that document. The text will appear onscreen as it is typed.

You don't have to issue carriage returns at the end of a line of text. Just keep typing until the end of a paragraph is reached. A feature called *word-wrap* will automatically break off the line when the cursor reaches the end of the onscreen line and will begin placing text on the next line down. You'll only need carriage returns to mark the end of a paragraph.

Loading a file into memory. Once you've started *Microsoft Word* running, you can load a text file from any drive/directory path. Simply select Transfer from the command bar, and then Load from the menu that appears. You'll be prompted for a filename. If you aren't sure of the filename, or if you want to see all the files available, press F1. You'll see a list of the files on the screen, with the first one highlighted. Press Enter to load this file, or use the cursor keys to highlight the file you want to load and then press Enter.

The *Microsoft Word* Load option is located under Transfer on the command bar.

A Quick Start with **Microsoft Word** *4.0*

- Activate the command bar with either the Esc key or the mouse.
- Press the T key, or move the mouse cursor to the word *Transfer* and click the left button.
- Now press L, or move the mouse cursor to the word *Load* and click the left button.
- Type in the name of the file to be loaded from storage on a disk. (If the file is not on the default drive, then be sure to include the drive name prior to the filename.) Then press the Enter key. The alternative is to press F1, which will display a listing of all document files available on the current drive. Move the highlight to the file you want to load and then press Enter.
- To escape without loading the file, press the Esc key.

The file will load into the computer's memory and will appear onscreen. Make any corrections, changes, additions, or deletions that are necessary. When everything is satisfactory, you may edit and save or print the file.

Printing the file. You don't have to save the file before you can print it. *Microsoft Word* prints a file directly from memory. You can type a document, print it, and then delete it if you don't want to save it. Or you can print one version, change the file in memory, and print another version.

Many word processors require that a file be printed from disk, but *Microsoft Word* allows printing a document from memory. The steps to print a file follow.

- Load the file into memory and make sure that it is as it should be.
- Activate the command bar by pressing the Esc key or using the mouse.
- Press the P key (for Print), or move the mouse cursor to the word *Print* and click the left button.
- When ready to start printing, press the Enter key.
- To escape without printing the file, press the Esc key.

When the file is through printing, the program will return to the edit mode. If you're finished with that file, either exit

29

Chapter 4

from the program or perform any other word processing functions desired.

Saving the file. Saving a file is very similar to loading it. The only difference, in fact, is that you select Transfer and then Save rather than Load. If your document is a new one, you'll have to provide a name for it.

The *Microsoft Word* Save option is located under Transfer on the command bar.

- Activate the command bar with either the Esc key or the mouse.
- Press the T key, or move the mouse cursor to the word *Transfer* and click the left button.
- Now press the S key, or move the mouse cursor to the word *Save* and click the left button.
- Type in the filename and press Enter.
- To escape without saving the file, press the Esc key.

This will save the file to the disk where *Microsoft Word* has been told to save text files. Unless otherwise specified, this will be the same drive used to boot up *Microsoft Word*. To specify another drive, include that drive's name preceding the filename

C:\ARCHIVE\TEXTFILE

You may add the extension .DOC, if you wish. If you don't, *Microsoft Word* will do it for you.

Limitations on filenames. Microsoft Word filenames are severely limited by the naming conventions of the MS-DOS operating system. If you create a great many text files, you'll have to use your imagination to avoid repeating filenames. You have to be careful to give every file a unique name. If there are two different files under the same name on different disks, and one is copied to the other's disk (which might happen when you are archiving rarely used files), the new file will overwrite the file on the disk.

Rules for naming a Microsoft Word *file.* The rules for naming a text file are simple, but they must be followed without variation. The computer will not accept a filename that does not fit the required format.

A Quick Start with Microsoft Word *4.0*

- A filename can be from one to eight characters long, using either numbers or letters.
- Don't use any other characters in the filename.
- Don't try to use blank spaces in a filename. *Microsoft Word* will not accept them.

Illegal characters. Several characters are illegal for use in a filename or extension. In this sense, the word *illegal* simply means you cannot use them. They have been reserved for special use by *Microsoft Word*. The program will not accept a filename with illegal characters. These characters are:

\
[
;
]
:
.
=
,
?
|
*

The DOC filename extension. A filename extension is nothing more than a suffix to add to a filename in order to lengthen or customize it beyond the mere eight characters allowed by MS-DOS. It is not necessary to add the DOC extension. *Microsoft Word* will add the extension automatically. This is how the program recognizes a document file when it prints a directory listing on the screen.

WYSIWYG

WYSIWYG is an acronym for *What You See Is What You Get*. *Microsoft Word* provides true onscreen formatting. The document will appear onscreen almost exactly as it will be printed. When a character is reformatted through the format mode, the change will be shown onscreen. This includes underlining and double underlining, italics, and boldface. The only shortcoming to this is that it does not show different sized fonts when you reformat the characters.

Chapter 4

Quitting the Program

It's simple to leave *Microsoft Word*.

- Activate the command bar with either the Esc key or the mouse.
- Press the Q key (Quit), or move the mouse cursor to the word *Quit* and click the left button.
- To save the changes before exiting, type Y.
- To abandon any changes, type N.
- To escape without quitting the program, Press the Esc key.

Chapter 5
Using the Transfer Menu

The term *transfer* may be confusing to you, particularly if you're used to word processors that rely on traditional computer terminology. Here the word *transfer* refers to data transfer: the manipulation of file data within a computer system.

While using *Microsoft Word*, you don't need to understand data transfer. For your purposes, simply remember that the Transfer menu refers to moving and manipulating text files.

What Is the Transfer Menu?

The Transfer menu contains most of *Microsoft Word*'s file data transfer commands. Each command acts on an entire document file at once. They move data from disk to disk, disk to memory, or memory to disk. The following table shows the functions of the options available from the Transfer menu.

Table 5-1. Transfer Commands

Command	Action
Load	Loads or copies a file from disk to memory.
Save	Saves or copies a file from memory to disk storage.
Clear	Clears text from the window or memory.
Delete	Erases files from a disk.
Merge	Joins files or parts of files into another.
Rename	Gives files a new name.
Glossary	Copies glossaries from one disk to another.
Options	Changes the Transfer source and target.

Loading a File into Memory

Loading means copying a file from the disk into the computer's memory. When you start *Microsoft Word*, it goes directly into the write-and-edit mode. Onscreen is a blank, unnamed text file ready for you to start typing. If you want to work on a file that already exists, you must load a copy of it into the computer memory.

Chapter 5 *LOADING*
A FILE

When you issue the Load command, you tell the computer to find the file on disk and then copy it into the computer's memory. When this is done, it'll appear in the text window onscreen. The file has thus been opened for writing and editing.

Loading a file with keyboard commands. Here are the steps for loading a file with keyboard commands.

- If you're working with multiple windows, use the F1 key to activate the window where the file is to be loaded.
- Press the Esc key, and type the letters *TL*.
- Press the F1 key to call the list of files in the currently logged drive and/or directory.
- Use the arrow keys to move the highlighting to your choice.
- If the text file is not in the source or directory, type in the filename. Don't forget to precede the filename with the drive name or directory.
- Press the Enter key.

Fast-loading a file. When you're first starting *Microsoft Word*, it's quicker to load a file with the keyboard instead of the mouse. This is because you can start typing as soon as the boot menu flashes onscreen, and *Microsoft Word* will remember your keystrokes. After you've loaded a few files, you'll begin to remember the necessary keystrokes. It's not necessary to wait for the prompt to begin typing. By contrast, to use the mouse, you must wait until the specified file appears on the screen to select it.

Loading a file with the mouse. Here are the steps for loading a file with a mouse.

- If you're working with multiple windows, put the pointer in the empty window and click the left button.
- Put the pointer on the word *Transfer* and click the left button.
- When the Transfer menu appears, put the pointer on Load and click the left button.
- Put the pointer on the highlight and click the right button. This calls the list. Use the mouse to make your selection.
- If the file is not on the list, you must type the filename. Don't forget to precede it with the drive or directory.

- Put the pointer on the words *Transfer Load* and click either button. Or press the Enter key.

Saving Your Files to Disk

When you save a file, the computer records a permanent copy of the words onto the disk. The basic technology involved is no different from recording music on a cassette.

Words typed onscreen are not permanent until you save them to a hard or floppy disk. They are only in the computer's memory. While a file is in memory, you may change, edit, and rearrange it any way you want.

But, while in memory, a text file is nothing but a pattern of electrons held temporarily in a weak magnetic field. It has no more substance than a puff of smoke. If you turn off the computer or lose your power supply, everything in computer memory will be erased.

Text in memory. The words onscreen are only being held in fragile electronic memory. Memory chips depend on a steady supply of carefully regulated electricity to keep working properly. Anything that interrupts the current flow can damage or erase your words from the memory chips. So your words are vulnerable to every change in the current supply.

This represents a very real danger. You are working in a real-world environment. Anyone can accidentally unplug the computer or turn off the power. Other electrical appliances on the same power line can transfer static to your computer system. Industrial users in your area can cause voltage spikes and power surges.

A *voltage spike* is a sudden, temporary jump in voltage. A *current surge* is an increase in power that comes when a heavy electrical user is suddenly turned off. Either of these can overload your computer and cause it to crash.

Protecting your work. The most important task you'll accomplish with a word processor is getting your work done. Second in importance is protecting what you've written so you won't have to type it over again. This is necessary because computer memory is very volatile. The best protection is to save a work file regularly and often. Get in the habit of saving files regularly; make it an important part of your work routine.

Chapter 5

Then, when an accident happens, all that will be lost is what you have typed since your last save. How often you save will determine how much of your work is at risk.

Save a file using the keyboard. The following steps use keyboard commands to save a file.

- If you're working with multiple windows, use the F1 key to activate the window where the file is to be loaded.
- Press the Esc key, and type the letters *TS*.
- The first time you save a file, you must give it a name. Type it, and give it the .DOC extension (if you forget to do this, the program will do it for you).
- Make sure that Formatted is set to *Yes*.
- Press the Enter key.

Speed saving. Here is a faster way to save files with keyboard commands.

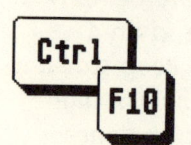

- Activate the window with the file to be saved.
- Hold down the Ctrl key and press the F10 key.

Save a file using the mouse. The following steps use the mouse to save a file.

- If you're working with multiple windows, put the pointer in the window where the file is to be loaded, and click the button.
- Move the pointer to the word *Transfer*; press the button.
- Move the pointer to the word *Save*; press the button.
- The first time you save a file, you must give it a name. Type it here, and give it the .DOC extension.
- Make sure that Formatted is set to *Yes*.
- Press the Enter key.

Guidelines for saving. Of course, how often you save and the number of backup copies of a file is up to you. Important material should be backed up often, and you should have plenty of copies. Less important material can do with less. Fifteen minutes is a good minimum interval between saves. Sav-

Using the Transfer Menu

ing more frequently than that is simply redundant. Thirty minutes is a good maximum interval between saves. You can type a lot of words in 30 minutes—you don't want to have to retype them.

Anytime you leave your keyboard, for any reason or for any length of time, save your file before you go. When your keyboard is unattended, anything can happen. If you can't remember how long it has been since the last save, save your file—it probably has been too long.

Anytime you come to a place where you need to stop and think, save the file. This can become a sort of punctuation to your writing. It's a way of saying, "There, I have that much finished."

Save the file before you close it to work on another. This will make sure that all changes are recorded. When you're quitting for the day, save the file in memory one more time just to make sure that you have saved any last changes you may have made. It's always better to be safe than sorry.

How to name a file. *Microsoft Word* text files are named according to MS-DOS file naming conventions. The rules are simple, but inflexible, and must be followed exactly. These rules are listed in Chapter 4. Basically, you may use any alphanumeric characters; that is, any letter of the alphabet or any numeral. Filenames can be from one to eight characters long, and they should be unique.

Giving files identical names. You can't have two files with identical names in the same drive and/or directory, but you can use filenames over and over again in different drives and directories. MS-DOS only reads one drive at a time. A different directory is functionally the same as a different drive.

The thing you have to be careful about is when you transfer files from disk to disk or from one directory to another. If there's already a file on a disk with the same name, the file coming in will write over the existing one, destroying it completely.

Microsoft Word will warn you if you try to give a file a name that's already used on the logged disk. The following message will display:

```
Enter Y to overwrite
```

37

Chapter 5

If you press Y, you'll delete the old file. One way to recycle useful filenames is to give them unique extensions.

Illegal filenames. There are four filenames that cannot be used, because they've been reserved by MS-DOS as names for devices. They can be used as extensions, however. These filenames are AUX, CON, PRN, and NUL.

Filename extensions. Filename extensions extend or lengthen a filename. Extensions are added to the filename with a period separating it from the filename. Extensions may consist of up to three alphanumeric characters.

Program files require filename extensions so that MS-DOS can know how to process them. *Microsoft Word* uses extensions to identify text files for the directory listing. Otherwise, they serve only as a personal convenience or as a coding device. But if you don't add an extension, *Microsoft Word* will add .DOC automatically.

Many *Microsoft Word* users find that an eight-character string is not enough to conveniently name all the files to be created. With a maximum of eight characters, it's difficult to avoid using filenames more than once. The solution is to add filename extensions to further customize the names. There are some reserved extensions that can't be used for ordinary document files: BIN, EXE, BAT, COM, and BAK. If you don't add an extension, *Microsoft Word* will add .DOC automatically. The file must have the .DOC extension to be displayed in the onscreen list.

An alternative to using extensions is to keep related files in a discrete disk or directory. Then it doesn't matter if filenames are repeated. Just be careful not to copy the file to the wrong place, because, if you do, it will write over and erase any file with the same filename.

Clearing Text from the Window or Memory

Microsoft Word allows you to open several text windows at the same time and work on a separate text file in each. The Transfer Clear command is used for clearing text files from these windows. You may clear either a specific document window or all of them at once. You don't have to clear the windows in

Using the Transfer Menu

the same order you opened them—clear them in any order you choose.

When you clear a window, you're removing the text in it from computer memory. So any changes not saved will be lost. If you've made any changes since the last save, the following message will appear at the bottom of the screen:

`Enter Y to save, N to lose edits, or Esc to cancel`

Clear with the keyboard. With the keyboard, you can either clear the window you are currently working in or clear all the windows currently open. These are your only choices. You cannot specify certain windows to be cleared.

- If you're working with multiple windows, use the F1 key to select the window you want to clear.
- Press the Esc key, and type the letters *TC*.
- Type *A* to clear everything, or type *W* to just clear the active window.
- You must save any changes you have made, or they'll be lost.

Clear with the mouse. Here are the steps for clearing the active window with the mouse.

- Activate the window to be cleared by putting the pointer into it and clicking the button.
- Put the pointer on *Transfer* and click the left button.
- Put the pointer on your choice and click either button.

Deleting Files from a Disk

When you delete a file, you're erasing its name from the directory and allowing *Microsoft Word* to use the space for something else.

The Transfer Delete command is used to erase text files from any drive or directory in the computer system. If you have a superfluous copy of a file on disk, or if you simply no longer need it, delete it.

Guidelines for deleting. There are important restrictions on what files you can delete.

39

Chapter 5

- You cannot delete the file on which you're currently working.
- You cannot delete any temporary files that have been created for *Microsoft Word* to use.
- If you try to delete a file that has been worked with in the current session, or any .TMP temporary file that *Microsoft Word* needs, then *Microsoft Word* will cancel the Delete command. Then it will display the message *Cannot delete file*.
- Before you can delete a text file that was open during the current session, you must issue the Transfer Clear All and then Transfer Delete commands.

Recovering deleted files. *Microsoft Word* has no built-in feature for recovering a deleted file. But utility programs are available that let you recover a file after it has been deleted. A very good one is *Norton Utilities*.

These programs work because the delete doesn't actually erase the file from the disk. Only the first character of the filename is deleted. Tagged to that first character are hidden codes that tell MS-DOS to display it on the directory, how to access it, and not to write over its text. Deleting the first character removes the file from the directory and takes away its write-protection. The utility program allows you to restore that first character to the filename.

If you're going to use a utility program to undelete a file, you must not write anything to that disk before you use the utility. The file's data has no write-protection, and any write function (such as saving or copying a file) can and probably will destroy it.

If you have a utility program that will undelete a file, but you don't know how to use it, do nothing with the computer until you get someone to help you.

The following steps will delete files from disk and/or directory.

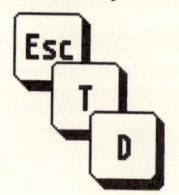

- Press the Esc key and type the letters *TD*.
- Press the F1 key to call the list of files.
- Use the arrow keys to move the highlight to the file to be deleted.
- If the file isn't on the list, you must type the filename and prefix it with the designated drive and/or directory.

Using the Transfer Menu

- Press the Enter key.
- Type *Y* to confirm the delete or *N* to escape without deleting.

Merging Files or Parts of Files into Another

When you merge one file into another, you're copying its text into the target file. With the Transfer Merge command, you join another file to the one you're working on. Once you know how to use it, this is the most time-saving feature of word processing.

When you have typed and saved text to disk, you never have to type that text again. Transfer Merge will copy that entire body of text into your document at the place you want it.

To merge an entire text file. The following steps are necessary to merge an entire text file.

- Put the cursor at the place in the current document where you want the merged text to appear.
- Press the Esc key and type the letters *TM*.
- If the file is on the list, press the F1 key to call it, and then make your selection.
- If the file isn't on the currently logged drive and/or directory, then you must type in the filename and prefix it with the designated drive and/or directory.
- Press the Enter key.

Renaming Files

The Transfer Rename command is used to rename the text file in an active window.

Renaming with the keyboard. The following steps allow you to use the keyboard to rename a file.

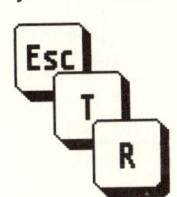

- Press the F1 key to activate the window with the file to be renamed.
- Press the Esc key and type the letters *TR*.
- Type the new name for the file. Don't forget the .DOC extension.
- Press the Enter key.

41

Chapter 5

Renaming with the mouse. The following steps allow you to use the mouse to rename a file.

- Move the pointer cursor into the window with the file to be renamed; click the left button.
- Move the pointer to the word *Transfer* and click the left button.
- Move the pointer to the word *Rename* and click the left button.
- Type in the new name of the file.
- Press the Enter key.

Transfer Glossary Commands

Glossaries are bits of reusable text that are stored in an archive and are drawn from as needed.

One of the best things about word processing is that, once something has been typed and saved to disk, you never have to type that text again. If you need it, you can simply call it from disk storage and merge it into any document where it is needed.

A glossary is a bit of text that you can use over and over again while writing standard documents. The most common use is to store standard paragraphs or specially formatted strings of numbers and letters that are awkward to reproduce by typing.

The Transfer Glossary options. There are three options under the Transfer Glossary commands: Merge, Save, and Clear. These act on an entire glossary file.

They work like the Transfer Merge, Transfer Save, and Transfer Clear commands but only affect glossary files.

When you run *Microsoft Word*, it loads the regular glossary file NORMAL.GLY into computer memory. Once you write a glossary and save it to this file, it'll always be available to you. This file stores the glossary entries you'll use during most of your write-and-edit sessions.

Glossary Merge. You don't have to use NORMAL.GLY (the default glossary file) exclusively. You can make as many special glossary files as you need to hold the glossaries for all your special purpose documents.

Using the Transfer Menu

Merging allows you to join your special-purpose glossaries with the ones in the default glossary file. If you have glossaries in other files saved under the same names, the ones merged in will replace the ones already in memory.

This merging can be either temporary or permanent. Usually it's temporary, intended to last only the duration of the current write-and-edit session. The merging is made permanent by saving NORMAL.GLY after the merging has been executed.

With the keyboard.

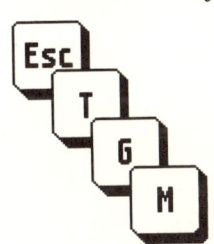

- Press the Esc key.
- Type the letters *TGM*.
- Press any arrow key to call the list of glossary files.
- Use the arrow keys to move the highlighting to the file of your choice.
- Press the Enter key.
- The second glossary file has been merged with the glossaries already in memory.

With the mouse.

- Use the mouse to select *Transfer*, *Glossary*, and *Merge*.
- To call the list of glossary files, move the mouse pointer to the small highlighted box after Transfer Glossary Merge and click the right button.
- Move the mouse pointer to the file of your choice and click the right button.
- The second glossary file has been merged with the glossaries already in memory.

Glossary Save. You may create glossaries strictly for use during a single write-and-edit session. When you turn off the computer, they'll be lost. But if you want to keep them so you may use again, you must save them.

Glossaries created during a write-and-edit session may be saved to NORMAL.GLY, the default glossary file. Or you may save them to any other file you wish to create.

43

Chapter 5

A glossary filename uses the standard naming convention, and it must have the .GLY extension.

With the keyboard.

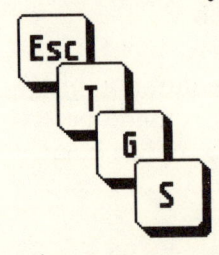

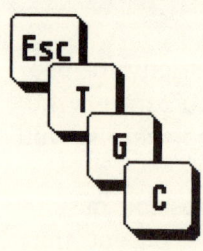

- Press the Esc key.
- Type the letters *TGS*.
- To save the new glossaries to the default glossary file, press the Enter key.
- To save them to a new glossary file, type in the correct drive name, directory path, and filename. (Remember to add the .GLY extension.) Then press the Enter key.
- The new glossaries are saved.

With the mouse.

- Use the mouse to select Transfer, Glossary, and Save.
- To save the new glossaries to the default glossary file, press the Enter key.
- To save them to a new glossary file, type in the correct drive name, directory path, and filename. (Remember to add the .GLY extension.) Then press the Enter key.
- The new glossaries are saved.

Glossary Clear. Clear means the same thing as delete. By using the Glossary Clear command, you can remove glossaries as easily as you create them. You can clear them all or clear them selectively from memory. This allows you to keep the glossaries updated and customized to your specific needs.

With the keyboard.

- Press the Esc key.
- Type the letters *TGC*.
- To clear all the glossaries, press the Enter key.
- To clear a specific glossary item, press an arrow key to call the glossary listing. Then use the arrow keys to move to the glossary item of your choice. Press the Enter key. Then type *Y* to confirm the delete.

Using the Transfer Menu

With the mouse.

- Use the mouse to select Transfer, Glossary, and Clear.
- To clear all the glossaries, press the Enter key.
- To clear a specific glossary item, press an arrow key to call the glossary listing. Then put the mouse pointer on the glossary item of your choice. Click the right button, and type Y to confirm the delete.

The Transfer Mode Options

There is only one command under Transfer Options. This allows you to change the setup for the default drive and directory path.

- Press the Esc key.
- Type the letters *TO*.
- Type the new drive and directory path.
- Press the Enter key.

Chapter 6
Using the Jump Mode

Microsoft Word has two different Jump commands. These are Jump Page and Jump Footnote (this indicates that Microsoft thinks you'll only use this particular command while working with footnotes or endnotes).

There's also an undocumented routine for jumping directly to the beginning or end of any active text window. It's described in the last section of this chapter.

Jump Footnote. The text for footnotes or endnotes is always inserted at the end of the current text file. When you insert a reference note with the automatic feature, *Microsoft Word* jumps to the end of the text file so you can type the note. When finished, you can jump back to the point where you were before inserting the reference note.

Jump Page. The Jump Page will take you directly to any specified page. The Jump Footnote command will go to either the next reference mark or directly to specified reference-note text at the end of the text file.

If you're going to insert and write a lot of reference notes in your document, it makes more sense to open a footnote window and toggle between the text window and the footnote window. This is much quicker than moving around in the text file.

But most people will use the Jump command to move around within the document. This accomplishes almost the same end as using Global Search to find your hidden text place-markers. The only catch is that you have to know what page you're looking for (on which page your target text is located).

Using the Jump Page Commands

The Jump Page command will not work if the document has never been paginated. The page numbers are assigned as a part of the printing routine. So a new document will not have

Chapter 6

page numbers until you print it or use the Print Repaginate command.

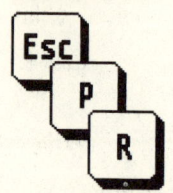

- Press the Esc key, and type the letters *PR*.
- Answer *Yes* or *No* at confirm page breaks. (The default is set to *No*.)
- Press the Enter key.
- *Microsoft Word* will go through the entire document, inserting page breaks and assigning numbers.

Assigning page numbers to divisions. Every division in a document can be numbered distinctly. The standard Print Repaginate command, as executed in the section above, will automatically repaginate and renumber every division in the document. If you don't want every division to be automatically renumbered, you must repaginate each division separately.

Jumping to a specific page. Nothing could be simpler than jumping to a specified page. Just call up the command and tell *Microsoft Word* to which page it should jump. When you call up the Jump Page menu, the current page will be displayed in the highlight. *Microsoft Word* will automatically search in the correct direction to jump to the specified page.

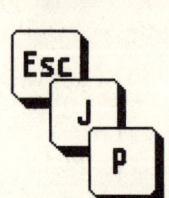

- Press the Esc key and type the letters *JP*.
- Type the page number to which you want to jump.
- Press the Enter key.
- *Microsoft Word* will jump to the first character at the top of the specified page.

For documents with multiple divisions. If the document has more than one division, there may be more than one page with the same number assigned. Each division in a *Microsoft Word* document can be assigned its own page numbers. This is done by marking the division with the highlight and then using the Print Repaginate command. You can jump to a specific page in a specific division by including the division number with the page number.

Using the Jump Mode

- Press the Esc key, and type the letters *JP*.
- Type the page number, then *D*, then the division number.
- Press the Enter key.
- *Microsoft Word* will jump to the first character at the top of the specified page in that division.

Speed page/division jumping. As with all the features that *Microsoft Word* considers important, there's a speed command or macro that will directly execute the function.

- Hold down the Alt key and then press the F5 key.
- Type the page number to which you want to jump.
- If there are divisions with their own numbering, type the page number, then *D*, then the division number.
- Press the Enter key.
- *Microsoft Word* will jump to the first character at the top of the specified page.

Using the Jump Footnote Command

The Jump Footnote command is a useful tool when rewriting or revising a document's reference notes. It'll take you directly to the reference-note text you need to check or edit. When you're ready, it'll jump you from the footnote text back to its reference number.

As stated earlier, the reference-note text is automatically collected at the end of the text file when you use the Format Footnote command. This is true whether you are printing them as footnotes or as endnotes.

Without this command, you'd have to jump to the end of the document and then scroll through the footnotes until you got to the one for which you were looking.

Jumping to a footnote. Here are the steps for jumping to a footnote:

- Put the cursor on the number of the footnote to which you wish to jump.
- Press the Esc key and type the letters *JF*.
- *Microsoft Word* will jump to the text of the footnote at the end of the document.

Chapter 6

Jump to the next reference number. If you don't position the cursor before issuing this command, then the above command will jump the cursor to the next reference-note number in the body of the document. Repeat the command, and you'll go to the reference-note text.

Jump back to the reference number. When you're finished checking or revising the footnote/endnote entry, *Microsoft Word* will let you jump back to the reference number in the body of the document.

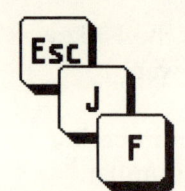

- Use the F9 or F10 keys to mark the entire reference note.
- Press the Esc key and type the letters *JF*.
- *Microsoft Word* will jump directly to the number of that reference note in the body of the document.

Jumping to Beginning or End

There's a simple routine for jumping to either the beginning or end of any document. This is not mentioned by Microsoft. The window must be active before this will work.

- Hold down the Shift key and then press the F10 key. This marks the entire text file with the cursor highlight.
- To jump to the beginning, press the up-arrow key.
- To jump to the end, press the down-arrow key.
- When *Microsoft Word* gets to either end of the document, the cursor highlight will be removed.

Part Two

Chapter 7
Copying, Deleting, and Inserting Text

This chapter begins with an overview meant to explain the basic revision techniques and to lead you to an understanding of what you need to do to edit and rewrite your documents with *Microsoft Word*. If you find more information than you need in the beginning, then skip over the first section. An overview should help you to understand, not get in your way.

The most significant factor in writing and editing documents with a word processor is that you can revise them without having to retype them from scratch. When documents are written by hand, or on a typewriter, you always leave behind a paper trail as you move from draft to draft of the manuscript. Revising a page, or even a single paragraph, can often mean having to retype an entire chapter of a book, a whole report, or an entire paper. But with a word processor, you create electronic documents that are in fact a stored body of text and data you can revise over and over again without wasting a single sheet of paper.

It's easy to revise documents with *Microsoft Word*—from correcting typing errors to checking spelling to rearranging entire paragraphs, pages, and sections. All you have to do is select the text to be revised, then issue commands and use word processing features. The computer will do the hard parts for you. Some of these commands are as simple as a single keystroke. Others are more complex and cumbersome, depending on how complex or difficult the task you are giving *Microsoft Word*.

Cut and Paste
There is one expression you'll hear over and over again in reference to word processing, and even in desktop publishing: *cut and paste*. It is a very visual term for describing what goes

Chapter 7

on during the revision of a document.

In the newspaper business, when copy was rewritten "off the wire," someone literally cut the teletype paper with scissors and pasted it back together with rubber cement. Sometimes a story could be assembled with pieces from both of the wire services. Sometimes the copy writer typed up something entirely new to add his or her personal touch. The result was a motley looking paste up, covered with proofreading symbols and corrections, that would be hand-carried to the typesetter.

Cut-and-paste is the technique of writing and editing a document by moving portions of a text file from place to place, or by combining existing text files or parts of those text files into the new documents you are writing. So you can assemble a document from building blocks, instead of having to type each word of it in place.

Revising documents with *Microsoft Word* eliminates the scissors, the rubber cement, the soft-lead pencil, and the dog-eared teletype or typewriter paper, but the process and the finished copy are essentially the same. You can take the first draft of any electronic document and make all the revisions or changes you need to make. But the process is clean and seamless. Everything is done with *Microsoft Word* commands and word processing features. It isn't effortless, and you still have to think hard about what you're doing. Yet the time and energy you save are well worth the trouble it takes to learn how to do cut and paste with *Microsoft Word*.

Copy, Delete, and Insert

Microsoft Word does not call this feature cut-and-paste. Instead, it calls the functions Copy, Delete, and Insert. The Copy and Delete commands have the capability of cutting blocks of text from electronic document and storing a copy of it temporarily in a special place in the memory *Microsoft Word* calls the *scrap*. Once text is stored in the scrap, then you can use Copy and Insert to put that text wherever you want it in that document or in another.

What is the scrap? The scrap is a special storage place set aside in the computer's memory for temporarily holding electronic text.

Copying, Deleting, and Inserting Text

Microsoft Word uses the scrap in two main ways: It holds the last deleted text in case you want to restore that text to the document, and it holds text sent by the Copy and Delete commands. It'll help if you think of the scrap as a scrap box for holding bits and pieces of text you have snipped out of the document. You can use these pieces again or throw them away.

The scrap will be empty when you first boot up *Microsoft Word*. It'll fill when you make your first deletion or copy procedure. From then on, anything you send to the scrap automatically replaces whatever was there before. The scrap will always retain the last text sent to it, until you exit from *Microsoft Word*. If you need to store more than one piece of text for later insertion, use the glossary feature.

The contents of the scrap are displayed between braces { } on the status line. This display is limited to 14 characters. If you send more than 14 characters to the scrap, the status line will display only the first 6 or 7 and the last 3 or 4 characters of the text in the scrap, separated by exclusion dots. See Figures 7-1 and 7-2.

Figure 7-1. Center Line of Text to be Deleted

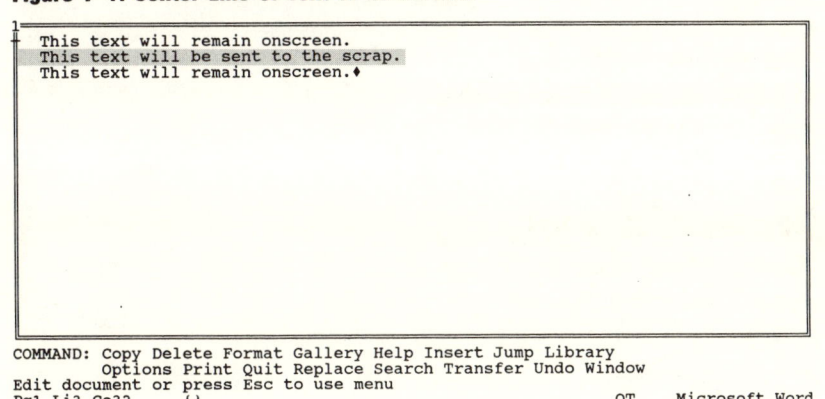

```
1
  This text will remain onscreen.
  This text will be sent to the scrap.
  This text will remain onscreen.◆




















COMMAND: Copy Delete Format Gallery Help Insert Jump Library
         Options Print Quit Replace Search Transfer Undo Window
Edit document or press Esc to use menu
Pg1 Li3 Co32      { }                              OT     Microsoft Word
```

55

Chapter 7

Figure 7-2. After Deletion, Line in Scrap

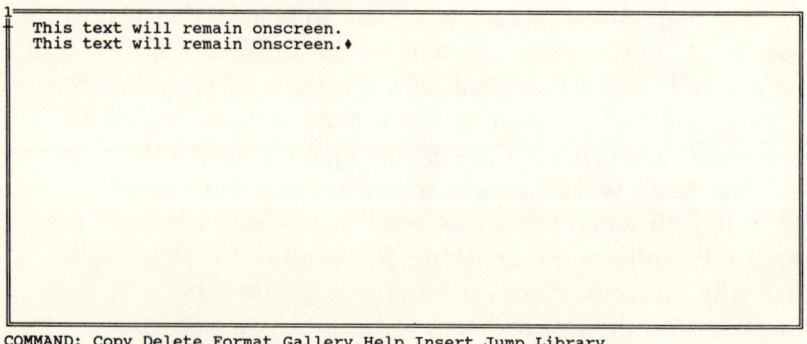

```
This text will remain onscreen.
This text will remain onscreen.♦
```

```
COMMAND: Copy Delete Format Gallery Help Insert Jump Library
         Options Print Quit Replace Search Transfer Undo Window
Edit document or press Esc to use menu
Pg1 Li2 Co1      {This·te...rap.¶}                OT    Microsoft Word
```

Symbols in the scrap. From time to time, you'll see some strange-looking symbols in the scrap. These are normally invisible characters *Microsoft Word* uses in the body of the text for performing word processing commands and functions. These symbols are high-bit ASCII characters. The scrap uses the symbols in the following chart to represent invisible characters.

Symbol Represents

‡	Automatic footnote numbers
☺	Automatic page numbers
↔	Beginning and end of hidden text
☻	Dateprint
§	Division mark
▪	End of row in column selection
↓	Newline character
—	Optional hyphen
¶	Paragraph mark
·	Space
→	Tab character
♥	Timeprint

Copying Text

When you copy text, you leave it in its original place in the document and transfer an electronic recording of it to another place in that document or to a document in another text win-

Copying, Deleting, and Inserting Text

dow. You might think of it as making a photostatic copy of a part of the text and inserting it elsewhere.

The Copy command on the command bar is part of the built-in cut-and-paste features of *Microsoft Word*. When you Copy text, you read it from a file onscreen and send it either to temporary storage in the scrap or to temporary or permanent storage in a glossary.

Copy text to another place. You can copy text from one place to another in the same document or you can copy text from one document to another in a different text window. These are the steps for using the command to copy text into the scrap.

- Select the text to be copied by expanding the cursor highlight to cover it. You can use either the keyboard or the mouse.
- Press the Esc key and type the letter C.
- Now press the Enter key to send the text to the scrap. You should see the first and last characters of the text between braces on the status line.
- Move the cursor to the place you want to copy the text. It can be in the same document or in one that's in another text window. (If you don't know how to use the windows for opening several text files at once, read the chapter on using windows.)
- Press the Ins key; the text will be copied.

You can also fast-copy the text by selecting it, press Alt-F3, move to the new location and press Ins.

Speed copying with the mouse. If you have a mouse connected to your system, there's a faster way to copy text. You don't have to send the text to the scrap beforehand.

- Expand the cursor highlight to cover the text you want to copy.
- Move the pointer to the place where you want to copy the text. It can be in the same document or in one that's in another text window. (If you don't know how to use the windows for opening several text files at once, read the chapter on using windows.)

Chapter 7

- Hold down the Shift key and then click the left button on the mouse.

Copy text with Delete. If you don't have a mouse, the fastest way to copy text is to use the Del key and Ins keys in a simple routine.

- Expand the cursor highlight to cover the text you want to copy.
- Press the Del key to send the text to the scrap and then press the Ins key to restore the text to its original location.
- Move the cursor to the place in the document where you want to make a copy of the text.
- Press the Ins key to copy the text from the scrap.

Copy to the glossary. If there's text in a text file that you want to use over and over again, you can copy it into storage in a glossary. By saving reusable text to glossaries, you're creating an archive of small text files. But if you're going to copy passages larger than the glossary can hold, you need to save that text to a file of its own. The glossary will accomodate very large pieces of text, however.

- Expand the cursor highlight to cover the text you want to copy to a glossary.
- Press the Esc key and type the letter C.
- Type in the glossary name under which you want to store the text.
- Press the Enter key. If you haven't tried to send it to a name that has already been used, that's all you have to do.

If you try to send text to a name already used for a glossary, *Microsoft Word* will ask you whether you want to overwrite the file or not. If you overwrite a file, the old glossary will be erased and the new information will take its place. If you don't want to write over the old glossary, answer *No* and try again. If you cannot remember what glossary names you've already used, press the F1 key to call up the list.

Copying text to a file of its own. You can use the Copy command to mark a block of text and save it to a file of its own.

Copying, Deleting, and Inserting Text

- Open a new text window and clear it of all text.
- Turn on the Window Zooming feature by holding down the Ctrl key and then pressing the F1 key. Zooming will display the text window full-sized onscreen. You can toggle between the two windows by pressing F1.
- Expand the cursor highlight to cover the text you want to copy to a file of its own.
- Press the Del key to put it into the scrap.
- Press the F1 key to toggle to the empty text window.
- Press the Ins key to retrieve the text from the scrap.
- Save the file under any legal filename.

Deleting Text

When you make a mistake while writing with a word processor, you don't have to grab an eraser to correct it. Just delete it from the screen and then type over it. If there's a sentence or paragraph or more in a text file that you don't want, then use a Delete command to remove it.

Remember that only the last saved version of the file is permanent. So the changes you make don't take effect until you update the copy on disk. If you realize you've made major deletions you'd like to put back, don't save the changed file. If you abandon the file without saving it, the previous version of the file will remain on disk. You can reload it and start over again.

Deleting to the scrap. When you delete text from a text file in memory, it will disappear from the screen. *Microsoft Word* sends that deleted text to temporary storage in the scrap (a buffer in RAM). The next word or sentence you delete will go to the scrap and replace what you deleted previously, and so on.

Inserting text from the scrap. It's inevitable—sometimes you'll delete text and then change your mind. Or you may accidentally delete the wrong thing. That is all part of the game. If you change your mind before deleting something else, you can put the text back simply by pressing the Ins key. The Ins key will insert the contents of the scrap into the document wherever you place the cursor.

Chapter 7

Deleting backward onscreen. *Microsoft Word* has been programmed to use the backspace key to delete backward from the cursor position. If you press it once, it'll delete one space or character to the left of the cursor. If you hold it down, it'll delete right-to-left continuously until you release the key.

Deleting forward onscreen. *Microsoft Word* has been programmed to use the Del key to delete forward from the cursor position. If you press it once, it'll delete one space or character forward. If you hold it down, it'll delete forward continuously until you release the key. You cannot delete past the end diamond.

Marking and deleting blocks of text. Deleting blocks of text with *Microsoft Word* is easier than with most word processors. Mark the text by covering it with the cursor highlight; then press the Del key. The marked text will vanish from the screen.

The cursor highlight can be expanded to cover any part of or all of the file. This is easiest to do with the mouse, where all you have to do is point, click, and drag the highlight over the text you want marked. But you can do the same thing with the keyboard.

Move your cursor to the beginning or the end of the section you want to highlight. Press F6 to begin highlighting a large block of text. The F7 key moves the highlight to the left from the current cursor position word by word. The F8 key moves the highlight to the right word by word. The F9 key moves the highlight backward through the text line by line. The F10 key moves the highlight forward line by line. Use the Shift key in conjunction with the arrow keys to expand the cursor highlight up, down, left, or right across large blocks of the text file. If you hold down the Shift key and then press the F10 key, it will highlight the entire file in memory.

Deleting without changing the scrap. There's one way to delete text permanently from a file in memory without sending it to the scrap. This will leave the contents of the scrap intact, and you can insert it where you need it.

Copying, Deleting, and Inserting Text

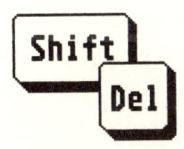

- Expand the cursor highlight to cover the text you want to copy to a glossary.
- Hold down the Shift key and press the Del key.

If you delete some text accidentally with this command, you can use the Undo command to recover it. You must do this before taking any other action.

Using the Delete Command

The slowest way to delete text is with the Delete command. The factory documentation says the command is meant to delete text to the scrap. But all deleted text goes to the scrap and stays there until you replace it by deleting something else. What the Delete command is actually useful for is to chop out scraps of text and save them permanently or temporarily to a glossary.

Deleting text to a glossary. You can delete short passages of text from your document directly into a glossary. By saving reusable text to glossaries, you create an archive of small text files. But if you want to delete larger passages than the glossary can hold, you'll have to save that text to a file of its own.

A glossary is actually a macro. A *macro* is a shorthand method of working with a word processor in which either command sequences or blocks of text are stored for later use. If you've typed something you know you're going to use over and over again, save it to a glossary where you can easily retrieve it later. Or, if you have to delete something from a text file you know you are going to need later on, you can delete it to a glossary from which you can call it when you need it.

- Expand the cursor highlight to cover the text you want to delete from the text file but save to a glossary.
- Press the Esc key and type the letter *D*.
- Type in the glossary name under which you want to store the text.
- Press the Enter key. If you haven't tried to send it to a name already used, then that's all you have to do.

61

Chapter 7

If you try to send text to a name already used for a glossary, *Microsoft Word* will ask you whether you want to overwrite the file or not. If you overwrite a file, the old glossary will erase and the new information will fill it. If you don't want to write over that old glossary, then answer *No* and try again. If you can't remember what glossary names you've already used, press the F1 key to call up the list.

Deleting text to a file of its own. If you need to delete a large or small portion from a text file, but know that you're going to need that text later, you can save that text to a file of its own before you delete it.

- Open a new text window and clear it of all text.
- Turn on the Window Zooming feature by holding down the Ctrl key and then pressing the F1 key. Zooming will display the text window full-sized onscreen. You can toggle between the two windows by pressing the F1.
- Expand the cursor highlight to cover the text to be deleted and saved to a file of its own.
- Press the Del key to erase the text and put it into the scrap.
- Press the F1 key to toggle to the empty text window.
- Press the Ins key to retrieve the text from the scrap.
- Save the file under any legal filename.

Moving and Inserting Text

When you move text in a document, it's deleted from its original place and then is inserted at a new location.

Moving text with Delete and Insert. The most common way to move text is to delete it from the old place, move the cursor to the place you want the text, and then insert it back into the file.

- Expand the cursor highlight to cover the text you want to move.
- Press the Del key.
- Move the cursor to the place in the document where you want to text to be.
- Press the Ins key.

Copying, Deleting, and Inserting Text

Moving text with the mouse. If you have a mouse installed, there's a fast way to move text around onscreen. This works only when moving text within the current screen page. You do not have to move text to the scrap before moving it where you want it.

- Expand the cursor highlight to cover the text you want to move.
- Move the cursor to the screen page where you want to move the text. Put the mouse pointer where the text is to be inserted.
- Hold down the Ctrl key and click the left mouse button.

Moving text to another document. If you need to move text from one text file to another, just follow the simple steps below. This process requires you to open another text window and use the Window Zooming command. If you don't know how to use these, read the section on using *Microsoft Word's* windows.

- If you aren't already working with multiple documents in multiple windows, open a new text window and load the second document into it.
- Turn on the Window Zooming feature by holding down the Ctrl key and then pressing the F1 key. Zooming will display the text window full-sized onscreen. You can toggle between two (or more) windows by pressing the F1 key.
- Toggle to the first window. Expand the cursor highlight to cover the text to be moved to the other document.
- Press the Del key to erase the text and put it into the scrap.
- Press the F1 key to toggle to the document in the other text window.
- Move the cursor to the place in that document where you want to move the text.
- Press the Ins key to retrieve the text from the scrap.

Inserting from a glossary with the Insert command. Once you have text stored in a glossary, it's easy to retrieve it and insert it at any place in any document you choose.

Chapter 7

- Put the cursor at the place in the document where you wish to insert the text stored in a glossary.
- Press the Esc key, and then type the letter *I*.
- Either type in the name of the glossary or press the F1 key to call up the list and use the arrow keys select it from the list.
- Press the Enter key.

Glossaries may be either temporary or permanent. If you want to keep glossaries permanent, you must save them before you exit *Microsoft Word*.

Chapter 8
An Introduction to Format Commands

When you type a document with *Microsoft Word*, it'll automatically format whatever you type to preset values. So, even if you only type and print, the document will have a readable and attractive appearance. *Formatting* controls the way text appears on the screen, and thus the way it appears on the printed page.

Microsoft Word has preset formats that allow you to type and print simple documents. You can change these formats to make your printed text look exactly the way you want it to look. These formats are changed either with the format commands or with command key sequences. The three basic types of text formatting are:

- Character
- Paragraph
- Page

The other formatting commands are extra features you can use to give your documents a more professional appearance. *Microsoft Word* displays text onscreen with the WYSIWYG approach. Within the limits of the monitor you're using, the graphics display shows you what the printed document will look like. Changing the appearance of the document onscreen means you're also changing the way the document will print.

The formatting commands give you a wide range of control over how your documents will look. If you have a laser printer, you can use *Microsoft Word* to produce camera-ready documents to send to your commercial printer or to use as-is for intracompany documentation and memos.

Chapter 8

The Default Settings

The preset formats of *Microsoft Word* are called the *default settings*. This means that they are settings the program will use each time you boot it up.

These can also be called the standard settings, because they will produce a standard "plain vanilla" document if you just type and print. The standard *Microsoft Word* settings are:

- Type that's 10-pitch (12-point), medium-weight.
- The first font on the list of fonts your printer driver will use.
- Left-aligned tab stops set every ½ inch.
- Standard 8½ × 11 inch paper. This is the size of sprocket-fed paper after the perfory (the strips of perforated paper containing the edge holes by which the paper is pulled through the printer) is torn off.
- Top and bottom margins that measure 1 inch.
- Left and right margins that measure 1¼ inches.

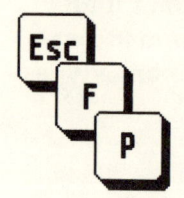

Checking the format of specific text. If you don't know, or don't remember, how specific text has been formatted, it's very simple to find out. Put the cursor on any paragraph of the text in question and then call up the menu for the specific type of formatting you want to check. The status of every format value will be displayed on that menu.

Changing the Format

Under the Options command on the command bar, *Microsoft Word* allows you to set the format measurements to use six different standards. All your measurements can be made in decimal fractions. You can set measurements in:

- Centimeters
- Inches
- Lines
- Pitch (10 or 12)
- Points

An Introduction to Format Commands

This allows you to print different documents to different standards—so you get the best use from whatever printer you happen to have. You can typeset the documents to fit what the printer can produce. Which measurement standard you use will depend on how exact you need to be in printing documents. If you're using *Microsoft Word* with a laser printer to produce camera-ready copy, you can use format commands for your documents as precise as you need.

Changing the measurement standard.
- Press the Esc key, and then type the letter O.
- Move the highlight to the measure selection.
- Put the highlight on the measurement option you want *Microsoft Word* to use.
- Press the Enter key.

Chapter 9
Formatting Characters

To *Microsoft Word*, characters are only special codes. When these codes are sent to the monitor screen, they're displayed as letters, numbers, and so on. When these codes are sent to the printer, the printer will interpret them and print the text.

How is *Microsoft Word* different from other programs? Word processing programs like *WordStar* show attribute changes by embedding printing commands onscreen. A special feature of *Microsoft Word* is that the character-attribute changes themselves are shown onscreen: Boldface is shown bold, italic is shown italic, and text underlined or stricken through shown that way onscreen.

The MS-DOS version of *Microsoft Word* does not have the true WYSIWYG capability of the Macintosh computer. It can't show perfect changes in font style or size on a regular monochrome or color monitor. But if you buy a WYSIWYG monitor and graphics card system like the Genius or the Amdek 1280, *Microsoft Word* is able to use their enhanced displays.

What happens during formatting? When you boot up *Microsoft Word* and start typing, everything you type is given the default formatting as "plain vanilla" text with no fancy tricks, no high-quality printing, nothing.

Character formatting tags the text with additional print codes that tell the printer to use special formatting on the printout. If you tag it with boldface, it tells the printer to make the characters darker. If you tag it with a larger size, it tells the printer to print larger. If you select a different font, it tells the printer to shape the characters differently.

Character tagging. For purposes of clarity, this book borrows the terms *tag* and *tagging* from *Ventura Publisher*, a high-powered desktop publishing program that's very easy to use and understand. They use the term *tagging* as a visual reference to the process of formatting the text.

Chapter 9

When you see the word *tag*, think of the paper tags you can tie to objects to identify them. In a metaphoric sense, that's what happens when you format characters, paragraphs, and page divisions. When you indicate text special-formatting, the codes are written into a tag that's attached to the selected text. The printer routine then reads the tag and produces a properly formatted printout.

There are many other similarities between *Ventura Publisher* and *Microsoft Word*. Every time *Microsoft Word* is updated, it moves closer to being a true desktop publishing program, narrowing the gap between them. Use the term *tagging* to help you understand the program, although you may see a variety of other terms used in Microsoft's documentation to convey the same concept.

Talking to the printer. When you change the format of the characters, you also change the coding that determines how the text will be printed. Depending on the printer you use, you may give many characters multiple tags. But many printers can print only a limited number of formats at the same time. If you give your printer too many things to do at once, it may print extremely slowly or may not perform all the required printing tasks.

Microsoft Word will use all the printers it supports to their fullest capabilities. It's up to you to know the capabilities of your printer and how to use them. If, for example, you're using a Hewlett-Packard LaserJet with the standard B cartridge installed, *Microsoft Word* will enhance every font on that cartridge. It'll be able to print italic Helvetica, boldface italic, and boldface eight-point Times Roman—whatever combination you like.

Formatting the Characters

When you change the character format, you can change the attributes, size, and type of font being used in the document.

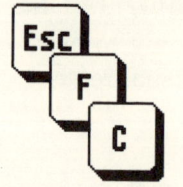

- Expand the cursor highlight to cover the characters to be reformatted.
- Press the Esc key and then type the letters *FC*.
- Use the mouse, or use the space bar and Tab keys, to move the cursor to select and set the character attributes you want to reformat.

Formatting Characters

- If you want to change the font being used or the size of the font, highlight the section you want to change and press the F1 key. (See Chapter 7 under the section on deleting text for instructions on highlighting text.) This will call up a list of the available fonts and font sizes. The fonts that are available for use depend on what printer *Microsoft Word* is currently installed to drive.
- When you have all the attributes set up as you want to format the marked text, press the Enter key. The format changes will be made onscreen.

The character tags options. When you call the format character menu, you'll see something that looks like Figure 9-1.

Figure 9-1. Format Character Menu

```
FORMAT CHARACTER bold: Yes No      italic: Yes No          underline: Yes No
        strikethrough: Yes No      uppercase: Yes No       small caps: Yes No
        double underline: Yes No   position: Normal Superscript Subscript
        font name:                 font size:              hidden: Yes No
Select option
Pg1 Li1 Co1          {}                                OT    Microsoft Word
```

There are 11 options on this menu. Seven of them control specific attributes of the characters. They are:

Bold. Use boldface to emphasize words or sentences in a document. The text will print in the normal boldface of the printer being used. With most dot-matrix printers, this will be in double- or triple-strike.

Italic. Use italic to give emphasis that's not as strong as boldface. Words from any foreign language should be put in italic. The text will print in the normal italic font of your printer. If you use a laser printer, *Microsoft Word* can add italic to all the fonts built into the printer or installed on a font cartridge.

Underline. Underlining can be used for emphasis. Use it to mark section or table headings or book titles in footnote references and bibliographies. The kind of printer you use determines whether the spaces between words will be underlined.

Double Underline. Double underlining will underline with two lines instead of one. As with single underlining, the

Chapter 9

kind of printer you use determines whether the spaces between words will be underlined.

Strikethrough. The strikethrough option is used to indicate text that should be removed or voided. This feature is often used in standard contracts or agreement forms for standard passages that are to be negated for that particular contract. These sections are marked through prior to signing the document in order to show variance from the standard.

Uppercase. This will automatically convert mixed-case text to all-uppercase text. This can be a great time saver: It eliminates having to retype the text. If you undo this change, the text will return to its previous mixed-case status.

Small Caps. This will automatically convert all mixed-case text into all small-capitals text. The formerly lowercase letters will be capitalized, but in a smaller size than the usual uppercase type. This eliminates having to retype the text.

Speed-formatting characters with Alt commands. If you don't like using the format character menu, you can bypass it by issuing Alt commands through the keyboard.

- Expand the cursor highlight to cover the text you want to have character formatted.
- Hold down the Alt key and press the letter key corresponding to the desired change.

For instance, if you wish to make a paragraph bold and underlined, highlight it by placing the cursor on the first character of the paragraph, hold down the Shift key, and cursor to the last character of the paragraph. Press Alt-B and then Alt-U. Press an unshifted cursor key, and the highlight will disappear to reveal the paragraph reformatted in bold and underline.

List of Alt format commands. Table 9-1 is a list of the Alt commands you can use to speed-format the characters in your documents. These commands can be used singly or in combination. However, some printers can only handle a few of

Formatting Characters

these commands at a time. If you give the printer more formatting than it can handle, it either will pick and choose which formatting commands to execute or will print very, very slowly.

Table 9-1. Formatting Alt Commands

Command	Effect
Alt-B	Boldface
Alt-I	Italic
Alt-U	Underlining
Alt-D	Double Underlining
Alt-K	Small Capitals
Alt-S	Strikethrough
Alt-E	Hidden Text
Alt-+ or Alt-=	Superscript
Alt- - (Hyphen)	Subscript
Alt–Space bar	Restore to Normal

Typing text in a new character format. You can also set the character format by issuing the above commands before you type the text on which you want to use special formatting.

- Hold down the Alt key and press the key for the character format you want to use.
- If you're using a style sheet, type X before the letter of the command.
- Type the text you want to format specially. It'll appear onscreen in the special formatting you have selected.
- When finished using that format, hold down the Alt key and press the space bar.

Changing text position. When text is printed, *Microsoft Word* tells the printer to feed the same length of paper for each line of text. The distance it feeds is the *set line height*. You can print text directly on the line or slightly above or below it.

The three types of text you may use are:

Normal. Normal puts text right on the line. This is what you should use for all regular printing.
Superscript. Superscript puts the marked text half a line above Normal text. This is used to set off footnote references,

Chapter 9

trademarks, and registered trademarks. It can also be used to show chemical, mathematical, and scientific formulas precisely.

Subscript. Subscript puts the marked text half a line below Normal text. This is used mainly in chemical, mathematical, and scientific formulas.

Using different fonts and sizes. The selection font name determines which font the printer will use to print the document. *Font* is the word that describes the design of the letters and other characters with which text is printed or displayed. The font name is the name of the particular design of an alphabet, like Times Roman or courier. *Microsoft Word* has six general categories of fonts, each with variations identified with a letter. So the font name is the category name plus the letter variant, as in *PicaD*. You can select fonts from a list *Microsoft Word* will display onscreen.

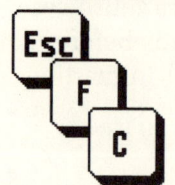

- Highlight this selection on the Format Character Menu.
- Press F1 to call up the list. The font styles on the list are determined by the printer driver *Microsoft Word* is currently set up to use.
- Use the arrow keys or the mouse to move the highlight to the desired font.
- Press the Tab key to go to another selection on the menu. Or press the Enter key to execute the format.

Changing font size. The *font size* is the height and width of the font, usually measured in points. Fonts are usually referred to by both name and size, as in 12-point Times Roman or 14-point Helvetica. *Microsoft Word* allows you to print your fonts in different point sizes. While on this selection, press the F1 key to call up the list. The font styles on the list are determined by the printer driver that *Microsoft Word* is currently set up to use. Use the arrow keys or the mouse to move the highlight to the desired font size. Then press the Tab key.

One way to use differently sized fonts in a document is to make section, chapter, and other titles larger than the rest of the document. You can even create a hierarchy of font sizes to

Formatting Characters

give your documents a special look. This helps the reader to visually divide subjects.

Hidden text. *Hidden text* is a character format that designates text as hidden or nonprinting. When you tag text as hidden, it'll display onscreen with an underline.

When the term *hidden* is used in this sense, it means that it's hidden from the printer. You can still see it on the screen. So, although you see the text onscreen, the printer will not print it as part of the document.

You can use hidden text for nonprinting annotations, for notes to yourself in the body of the document, for a table of contents, and for index codes. Long-time users of *Microsoft Word* will recognize hidden text as being almost the same thing as the embedded comments commonly used in that program.

Tagging text as hidden. The following steps cause text to be changed to hidden (nonprinting) text:

- Use the function keys or the mouse to mark the text to be tagged as hidden.
- Press the Esc key and type the letters *FC*.
- On the Format Character menu, answer *Yes* at the hidden text prompt.
- Press the Enter key.
- The text will be displayed as dot-underlined text.
- If the text disappears when you tag it as hidden, the hidden text display on the Widow Options menu is toggled off.

Double-hidden text. It's possible to double-hide text within your documents. This may sound a bit confusing, but it isn't. After your text is formatted as hidden, you can then choose whether to display the hidden text onscreen.

When hidden text is displayed, it appears as underlined text. If you choose to double-hide text, it simply doesn't appear onscreen at all. It vanishes from the screen, and the text after or below it moves up and over, filling in the space the hidden text used to fill. But don't think the text has been deleted—it's still there.

Chapter 9

Double-hiding the text. This option is found in the Window Options menu. These steps will double-hide your text:

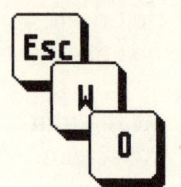

- Press the Esc key and type the letters *WO*.
- Answer *No* to the command Show Hidden Text. If you have this display toggled off, the hidden text will disappear from the screen when you format it as hidden.

In order to remove the hidden formatting from text, you must have it displayed onscreen so that you can mark it with the cursor highlight. It's simple to display hidden text. Simply follow the same steps above, but respond *Yes* to the Show Hidden Text command.

Deleting hidden text. When hidden text is displayed onscreen, you can delete it just like any other text. When hidden text in the body of text is sent to the scrap or to a glossary, it'll be copied there and removed from the body of the text.

When hidden text is in the body of a block of text you delete, it'll be deleted as well. Be careful not to unintentionally delete double-hidden text.

To remove an entire paragraph or more of hidden text, mark it with the cursor highlight and press the delete key.

Editing hidden text. When hidden text is displayed onscreen, you can edit, rewrite, and add to it just as you would any other text in the document. Just put the cursor where you want to add text or make changes.

When text is double-hidden, you cannot edit it.

Chapter 10
Formatting Paragraphs

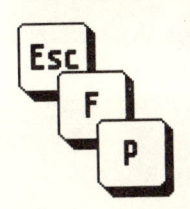

As far as *Microsoft Word* is concerned, a paragraph is any text up to and including the paragraph mark. In the course of working with a document, this means that a paragraph is anything that falls between two carriage returns.

Paragraph formatting tags are printing codes attached to the paragraph mark. These tell *Microsoft Word* how to display the paragraph onscreen. They also tell the printer how to print the paragraph on the page.

A new paragraph is begun by pressing the Enter key. This inserts a carriage return in the document. If you just boot up *Microsoft Word* and start typing, it'll use the default paragraph formatting. This results in "plain vanilla" paragraphs with no special formatting at all. If you want more customized printing, you can format paragraphs as you type them or go back later and reformat them as a part of revising the document.

Formatting Paragraphs

When you set the paragraph format, you tell *Microsoft Word* how to shape and print the paragraphs. You do this by tagging the paragraphs with formatting codes. These control paragraph alignment, line spacing, left and right indention, and the blank space used to separate paragraphs. Figure 10-1 shows the Paragraph Format menu.

Figure 10-1. The Format Paragraph Menu

```
FORMAT PARAGRAPH alignment: Left Centered Right Justified
      left indent:              first line:         right indent:
      line spacing:             space before:       space after:
      keep together: Yes No     keep follow: Yes No side by side: Yes No
Select option
Pg1 Li1 Co1       {}                                OT     Microsoft Word
```

Chapter 10

You can give every paragraph the same formatting throughout a document. Or you can give each paragraph a custom format as needed. Your goal is to make the text fit the needs of the document.

Different kinds of documents demand different kinds of paragraph formatting. There are personal standards, company or corporation standards, and national standards. For every document, there are paragraph formats that work best and get the job done. If the default settings are not what you need to get your work done, you must learn how to reset and customize *Microsoft Word*. The program can be customized to meet the needs of any documentation.

To format the paragraphs correctly, you need to know how the documents should appear when printed. A good stylebook or writing handbook can help you with that. You might consider *The Harbrace College Handbook, The Chicago Manual of Style,* or *The Secretary's Handbook*. There are many other good ones on the market. If your company has its own stylebook, you'd be wise to learn it thoroughly.

Using the Paragraph Format Features

You can use either the function keys or the mouse to mark paragraphs for formatting.

- To select one paragraph for formatting, simply put the cursor anywhere on the paragraph.
- To mark multiple paragraphs for formatting, cover the paragraphs with the cursor highlight.
- To mark all the paragraphs in a document for formatting, hold down the Shift key and press the F10 key.

Selecting paragraph format changes. These steps can be used to change the formatting on any single paragraph, a group of paragraphs, or an entire document. If you have a mouse, use it to go directly to the paragraph tags you want to set.

Formatting Paragraphs

- Mark the paragraphs for formatting.
- Press the Esc key and then type the letters *FP*.
- Use the space bar and Tab keys to move the cursor around on the menu. Set them as they should be.
- Press the Enter key.

Elements of Paragraph Formatting

The following options are available with the Format Paragraph command. They'll be discussed in greater detail later.

Alignment. This is the term Microsoft uses to describe the justification status of the paragraph. (While *alignment* is technically correct, *justification* is the more commonly used term.) Text can be right-justified, left-justified, center-justified, or fully justified. The default setting is left-justified.

Left Indent. A left indent is any additional space the text is moved in from the left margin. The default left margin is one inch. The default left indent is zero. You can't use negative numbers to create a left outdent.

Right Indent. A right margin is any additional space the text is moved in from the right margin. The default right margin is one inch. The default right indent is zero. You can use negative numbers to create an right outdent.

First Line. This sets the paragraphs to indent automatically when you start typing the first line of the paragraph. The default setting is zero. If you don't use this at the beginning of the document, you can always go back and reformat the paragraphs with this indent. You can use the tab key to perform paragraph indents.

Line Spacing. This is the space automatically inserted between lines of text. The default line spacing is 1, but Microsoft mentions no limitations on how wide you can set the line spacing. You can use any of the measurement standards to set line spacing and can put them as far apart as you want them.

79

Chapter 10

Space Before. This is the blank space automatically inserted before the beginning of the text in the paragraph. It controls the space between paragraphs without the use of carriage returns. The default setting is zero.

Space After. This is the blank space automatically inserted after the last text in a paragraph. It controls the space between paragraphs without the use of carriage returns. The default setting is one line.

Keep Together. This is used to keep a paragraph together when it normally would be separated at a page break and printed on separate pages. If there isn't enough room at the bottom of the page for the whole paragraph, it'll be printed on the next page. The default setting is No.

Keep Follow. This is another way of controlling the automatic page breaks. It keeps two paragraphs together. If there isn't room at the bottom of the page for at least two lines of the second paragraph, it and the last two lines of the first paragraph will be moved.

Side by Side. This tags the paragraphs for side-by-side printing. There are two methods for printing paragraphs in the side-by-side format, and this method is more difficult than the other. But it will give you more precise control over paragraph positioning.

Paragraph Justification

There are four different kinds of alignment or justification for your paragraphs: left, center, right, and fully justified. These control how the lines of text fit between the margins.

Left justification. The most commonly used paragraph alignment is left justification. This justifies the lines of text against the left margin only. It makes a smooth left margin and a ragged right margin.

Right justification. The least commonly used paragraph alignment is right justification. The lines of text are justified against the right margin only, making a smooth right margin and a ragged left margin. It can be very difficult to read.

Formatting Paragraphs

Center justification. This centers all the lines in a paragraph between the currently set margins. This is useful for headings, titles, and text that need to stand out from the text above and below it. Both margins will be ragged.

Full justification. This justifies the lines of text against both margins. Varying spaces are added between words to make each line exactly the same length. Both margins are smooth.

Hyphenation with full justification. If you're going to do standard incremental printing, you should definitely use hyphenation with full justification. When full justification is used, word-wrap breaks a line off when a word passes the right margin and then adds incremental spaces to lengthen the line. With incremental printing, this results in lines with large gaps between the words. By hyphenating the document, you can reduce the size of blank space and print more text on each line. To select hyphenation:

- Press the Esc key, then L.
- Highlight Hyphenation and press Enter.

Controlling Indention

Microsoft Word supports three types of indention: left indent, right indent, and first-line indent.

Left Indent. Any additional space the text is moved right from the left margin is left indention. The default left margin is one inch. The default left indent is zero. You cannot use negative numbers to create a left outdent.

Right Indent. Any additional space the text is moved left or right of the right margin is right indention. The default right margin is one inch. The default right indent is zero. You can use negative numbers to create an right outdent.

First Line. This is for automatic paragraph indention. If you select this option when you begin the document or paragraph, paragraphs will indent as you start typing them. You

81

Chapter 10

can always go back and reformat the paragraphs with this indent. The default setting is zero. You can use negative numbers to print outdents. You can also use the tab key to manually indent paragraphs.

Marking paragraphs for indention. Use either the mouse or the function keys to select the paragraphs to be indented. The text window must be active for the function keys to work.

- To mark a single paragraph, simply place the cursor anywhere in the paragraph you want to indent.
- To mark more than one paragraph, expand the cursor highlight to cover the paragraphs.
- To mark all the paragraphs, hold down the Shift key and press the F10 key.

Setting left indention. Paragraphs can be indented anywhere to the right of the left margin. Don't set the left indent past the current right margin. Use any of the measurement standards (Table 10-1). You cannot use negative numbers to create a left outdent. You can set a right indent at the same time.

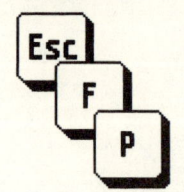

- Mark the paragraphs to be given this particular left indent.
- Press the Esc key and then type the letters *FP*.
- At left indent on the Paragraph Format menu, type the size number of the indent. If using a measurement standard other than the preset one, you must include its symbol (see Table 10-1).
- Press the Enter key.

Table 10-1. Symbols to Specify Format Measurement

Symbol	Measurement
cm	Centimeters
in (or ")	Inches
li	Lines (1/6 inch)
pt	Points (1/72 inch)
p10	10-pitch characters
p12	12-pitch characters

Formatting Paragraphs

Setting right indention. Paragraphs can be indented anywhere to the left or right of the right margin. Don't set right indent to the left of the current left margin. Use any of the measurement standards (see Table 10-1). Use negative numbers to create an outdent. You can set a left indent at the same time.

- Mark the paragraphs to be given this particular right indent.
- Press the Esc key and then type the letters *FP*.
- At right indent on the Format Paragraph menu, type the size of the indent. If you're using a measurement standard other than the preset one, include its symbol.
- Press the Enter key.

Hanging indents. Hanging indention causes the body of the text to hang away from the normal margins. This makes the hanging text visually distinctive in appearance from the surrounding nonindented text.

There are two ways to set hanging indents. The first is to highlight the paragraph and use the standard indention routines described above to set left and right indents. Another way to set hanging left indents is with the Alt-T command.

Hanging indents give numbered lists, bullet lists, lists of definitions, or bibliography entries an attractive and distinctive appearance. The text in the list hangs away from the number or bullet that designates it.

Hanging indents are also used to make a paragraph stand out from the text around it. This is the usual format for including long quotations in a research paper, thesis, or dissertation.

    Hanging indents are used to move text over from the right or the left margins for emphasis or to make room for illustrations, charts, or tables to be pasted in during or after typesetting. This paragraph has hanging indents.

Speed-set hanging left indents. Microsoft Word has an Alt command that can be used to indent your paragraphs quickly. This is the quickest way to format hanging indentions:

Chapter 10

- Mark the paragraphs to be given a hanging indent.
- Hold down the Alt key and and then type the letter *T*.
- Each repetition of Alt-T will move the hanging indention one additional tab setting to the right.

Paragraphs indented with Alt-T will retain whatever other alignments you have already given them. You can change the justification without losing the hanging indent.

Indenting Alt commands. Table 10-2 is a list of the Alt commands you used to indent paragraphs for stepped indention. The procedure for all commands is to highlight the paragraphs to be indented, hold down the Alt key, and type the letter of the command.

Table 10-2. Indenting Alt Commands

Command	Effect
Alt-F	First-line indent increased by one tab stop.
Alt-N	Left indent increased by one tab stop.
Alt-M	Left indent decreased by one tab stop.
Alt-T	Creates hanging indent. Indent increased by one tab stop.

Stepped indents. Stepped indents create the visual effect of steps going up and down in the body of the text. You can step indent:

- By moving the left margin toward the right.
- With standard hanging indention.
- By varying the first-line indention.

Stepped indents are used for setting off paragraphs by indenting them selectively according to the content or purpose of the text in the paragraph. With stepped indents, you can set off subordinate text—like long quotations, notes to the reader, or tips—by giving them their own level of indention. Paragraphs can be step-indented according to their relative status in the document.

Indenting with the mouse. The mouse can be used to set left, right, and first-line indents. This process requires calling the Format Paragraph menu. This is slower than using the Alt commands, but it allows you to make your changes by point-and-click.

Formatting Paragraphs

If you don't have the ruler line on already, calling this menu will make it appear on the top edge of the text window. The indention symbols already tagged to the paragraphs will be displayed.

- Mark the paragraphs to be indented.
- Select Format Paragraph.
- Put the mouse pointer on the symbol (on the ruler line) for the tab you wish to change (see Table 10-3).
- Hold down the right mouse button.
- Drag the symbol to the new location on the ruler line and release the button.
- The indent symbol will move with the cursor. You can use the mouse to make other indent changes to the ruler or to any other selection on the menu.
- To make the indents effective, press the Enter key.

Table 10-3. Indention Symbols on the Ruler Line

Symbol	Type of Indent
[	Left indent
]	Right indent
I	First-line indent

Guidelines for indent display. One of the weaknesses of *Microsoft Word's* graphics display is its inability to display both of two different symbols that occupy the same location on the ruler line.

The left indent and first-line indent often occupy the same position. When their symbols overlap on the ruler line, you'll only see the left-indent symbol ([).

If you want to see and change the first-line indent symbol, then you'll have to move the left indent symbol. When you're finished moving the first-line indent, you'll have to put the left-indent symbol back in its place.

If you have any tab stops set, their symbols (L, C, R, D, and I) will hide indent symbols.

Restore default indention. If you just want to remove left and right indents, it's best to use the Format Paragraph menu and set everything back to the defaults. The Alt-P command will return paragraphs to default formatting. But this also removes all other formatting.

Controlling Spacing

In general, there are three types of spacing:

- Automatic space between lines in a paragraph.
- Automatic line-space before a paragraph.
- Automatic line-space after a paragraph.

Setting Line Spacing. Line spacing is a selection on the Format Paragraph menu. The default line spacing is one line (single-spaced), but you can use any measurement standard. There's essentially no limit on line spacing.

- Highlight the paragraphs to be formatted with a different Line Spacing.
- Press the Esc key and then type the letters *FP*.
- At Line Spacing, type the value in lines (li) you want to use for Line Spacing. You can also use inches (in or ") or points (pt).
- Press the Enter key.

Microsoft Word's default line spacing is one line or 12 points. This allows six lines per inch. You can decrease line spacing and print—for example, having eight or more lines per inch—by typing a line-space setting in points smaller than the default. To get eight lines per inch, type 0.125" or 9 pt.

Speed-set double-spacing. If you want to bypass the menu and set Line Spacing to double-spacing, you can do so with an Alt command. This command is very limited because you can only set double-spacing with this command.

- Highlight the paragraphs to be formatted with a different line spacing.
- Hold down the Alt key and type 2.

Restore single-spacing. If you want to remove double-spacing, it's best to use the Format Paragraph menu. The command Alt-P will return paragraphs to single-spacing, thus restoring default formatting. But this also removes all other extra formatting as well.

Formatting Paragraphs

Paragraph-spacing guidelines. Paragraph spacing is the amount of blank space inserted between paragraphs in a document. *Microsoft Word* allows you to decide whether there is to be blank space and to control precisely how much space is inserted.

There are three different ways to control the space between paragraphs:

- Manually
- Automatic placement of a Space Before
- Automatic placement of a Space After

The last two methods will automatically insert the space you set between paragraphs. In most cases, you'll use only one or the other. Default paragraph spacing is set in lines, but you can use any of the other measurement standards. Generally, use the Space Before option to set one blank line before your regular paragraphs and use the Space After option to set one or more blank lines after special paragraphs, titles, section titles, or other headings.

Manual paragraph spacing. Many simple documents, like letters and memos, do not require blank spaces between paragraphs. To use manual spacing:

- Set Space Before and Space After to 0.
- Use the Enter key to issue carriage returns.

Set Space Before. The following steps will cause an extra line to be inserted ahead of all paragraphs:

- Mark the paragraphs to be formatted with automatic spacing.
- Press the Esc key and then type the letters *FP*.
- At Space Before, type the number of blank lines you want between paragraphs. (This measurement can also be set in inches (in or ″) or points (pt).
- Press the Enter key.

Chapter 10

Set Space After. The following steps result in a similar effect, but insert the extra line after rather than before each paragraph:

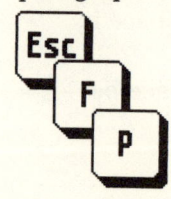

- Mark the paragraphs to be formatted with automatic spacing.
- Press the Esc key and then type the letters *FP*.
- At Space After, type the number of blank lines you want between paragraphs. (This measurement can also be set in inches or points.)
- Press the Enter key.

Controlling Widows and Orphans

Widows and orphans are two common problems when printing documents. When a paragraph begins very near the end of a printed page, you'll see widows and orphans. A *widow* occurs when all but one line of a paragraph appears on the previous page. The single line at the top of the page is a widow. Similarly, a paragraph may begin printing on the very last line of a page, leaving a single line at the bottom of the page and the rest of the paragraph on the next page. The single line is an *orphan*.

Widows and orphans give documents awkward paragraph breaks that detract from a professional appearance. There are three different ways to control this printing problem:

- Manual control
- Keep Follow
- Automatic Widow/Orphan Control

Manual control. *Manual control* means that you simply watch where the page breaks fall when you repaginate the document.

- If you see an orphan onscreen, insert carriage returns until the orphan moves below the page break. Then repaginate again if necessary.
- If you see a widow onscreen, insert a page break higher in the paragraph. If the paragraph is only a few lines long, put the page break above the paragraph and repaginate if necessary.

Formatting Paragraphs

Keep Follow. The second method is to use the Keep Follow option on the Format Paragraph menu. This is the option that forces paragraphs to be printed on the same page. It will allow paragraphs to be broken, however, after the second line of the second paragraph or before the second-to-last line of the first paragraph. In other words, if the first two lines of the second paragraph can't fit at the bottom of the current page, the last two lines of the first paragraph will be printed at the top of the next page.

Automatic widow and orphan control. *Microsoft Word* has a feature that will automatically control widows and orphans. Found on the Print Options menu, it's called *widow/orphan control*. It operates during the print run-off. If there isn't enough room on the page for the entire paragraph, the whole paragraph will be moved to the next page. If printing text in columns, the paragraph will move into the next column.

This is a brutal way to control widows and orphans. The smallest unit it can measure is a paragraph. It doesn't count lines, and it won't simply shift the page (or column) break to eliminate the basic problem.

Automatic widow and orphan control will make awkward breaks that leave too much empty space at the bottom of a page. If page count is important, or if you want to print a constant number of lines on each page, you're better off controlling this manually or with the Keep Follow option.

Another flaw in automatic widow and orphan control is that it can break apart other text that you want to keep together. This can be in the middle of a table, a list, or a paragraph that will lose effectiveness if split between two pages.

Keeping Text Together

There are occasions when it's essential to keep text in a paragraph on the same page. Sometimes information is so important it must be seen together to avoid mistakes.

Normal pagination or repagination will break a document into pages at regular intervals regardless of where it splits paragraphs or lines of text.

Chapter 10

When automatic widow and orphan control is turned on, it can also break apart other text that must be kept together. This can happen in the middle of a table, a list, or a paragraph that will lose effectiveness if split between two pages.

The Keep Together command. To prevent this, use the Keep Together command on the format paragraph menu.

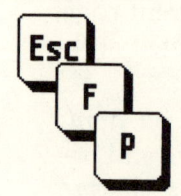

- Mark the paragraph to be kept together during the print run-off.
- Press the Esc key and type the letters *FP*.
- At Keep Together, answer *Yes*.
- Press the Enter key.

The Keep Follow command. This is used to keep the page break from falling between two paragraphs. If the first two lines of the second paragraph can't fit at the bottom of the page, the last two lines of the first paragraph will be printed at the bottom of the next page. This is useful to prevent a heading from printing as a single line at the bottom of a page.

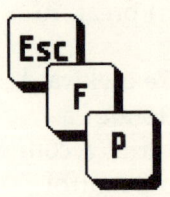

- Put the cursor anywhere on the the first paragraph of the pair.
- Press the Esc key and type the letters *FP*.
- At Keep Follow, answer *Yes*.
- Press the Enter key.

Speed-Formatting Paragraphs

As with character formatting, you can use Alt commands to speed-format paragraphs in your documents. This means you can bypass the Format Paragraphs menu and reformat without leaving the typing mode.

- Mark the paragraphs to be reformatted.
- Hold down the Alt key and and type the code letter for the format(s) you want to use. If a style sheet is attached to the document, you must type the letter X before typing each of the letters of the Alt command.

Formatting Paragraphs

- As you type the letter(s) of the command(s), *Microsoft Word* will automatically shape the paragraph to fit the new format(s).

You can go back later to insert to or delete text from that paragraph. *Microsoft Word* will automatically correct the paragraphs to keep them within the assigned format.

You can use more than one paragraph format by typing each Alt command letter in sequence. But if you try to use formats that contradict one another, *Microsoft Word* will go with the last one you typed in the sequence.

Speed-formatting as you type. As with character formatting, you can use Alt commands to speed-format paragraphs as you type them into your documents. To use these directions, you must have Options Display set to either partial or complete.

- You haven't pressed the Enter key at the end of the paragraph. If you want to speed-format, from the beginning of a new document, issue a carriage return. Then put the cursor back on the paragraph mark.
- Hold down the Alt key and type the letter(s) of the formatting command(s) you want to use. If you are using a custom style sheet, you must type the letter *X* before the format command letter.
- Now just type the paragraph. *Microsoft Word* will be set to use the new paragraph format for everything you type until you change it again.

When you get to the end of the paragraph, issue another carriage return. The new paragraph will have that same format tagged to it. If you use the arrow keys to move up or down past those paragraphs, *Microsoft Word* will revert to the formatting of the paragraph to which you move.

List of Alt paragraph format commands. Table 10-4 is a list of the speed-formatting commands that can be executed with the Alt key.

Table 10-4. Alt Paragraph Format Commands

Command	Effect
Alt-C	Center-formats paragraph
Alt-L	Flush-left paragraphs
Alt-R	Flush-right paragraphs
Alt-J	Fully justified paragraphs
Alt-F	First-line indent of paragraphs
Alt-M	Decrease indention on paragraphs
Alt-N	Increase indention on paragraphs
Alt-O	Put blank space between paragraphs
Alt-P	Restore normal or default paragraphs
Alt-T	Hanging indention on paragraphs
Alt-2	Double-space paragraphs

Copying Formatting

If you have set up a pleasing format for a character or a paragraph and you want to use it elsewhere, the quickest way to accomplish this is by copying the format.

Copying character-formatting with the mouse. The following steps will allow you to format text with the mouse.

- Put the mouse pointer on a character that has the format you want to copy.
- Hold down the Alt key.
- Click the Left Button.

Copying paragraph-formatting with the mouse. You can also copy paragraph-formatting with the mouse. Follow these steps:

- Expand the cursor highlight to cover the paragraph whose format you want to copy.
- Hold down the Alt key.
- Click the Left Button.

Repeat formatting. *Microsoft Word* has a shortcut you can use for repeating the formatting of any paragraph you have just changed. A repeat last command is installed on the F4 key.

Formatting Paragraphs

- **F4** • After you format either characters or paragraphs, mark the next text that you want to format exactly the same way.
- Press the F4 key.

The F4 key simply repeats whatever last command action you took. So this will only work if you do it before executing any other commands. And if you have applied multiple formats with Alt commands, F4 will only repeat the last one.

Repeat formatting with the mouse. The action described above is also possible with the mouse. Follow these steps:

- After you format either characters or paragraphs, mark the next text that you want to format exactly the same way.
- Put the mouse pointer on the word *Command:* on the command bar; click the left button.

Printing Columns Side by Side

Side-by-side printing will print consecutive paragraphs in a two- or three-column format. One example of this would be interviews or other question-and-answer documents. With side-by-side printing, you can put the questions on the left and the answers on the right.

Another use would be in pamphlets or other documents describing a product. Print product features in one column and the uses of those features in the other.

Paragraph sets. Paragraphs are said to be in *sets* when they are aligned at the same level on a page. If a set is too long to fit on the bottom of the page, *Microsoft Word* will print them entirely on the next page.

With *Microsoft Word*, you can align up to 32 consecutive paragraphs in side-by-side formatting. This side-by-side alignment only works within the body of the printed page. You cannot format side-by-side footnotes, headers, or footers.

Displaying side-by-side paragraphs. The paragraphs do not display side by side onscreen, but they'll align correctly when printed. Paragraph sets will display in their true column width, but in a staggered display instead of true side-by-side. *Microsoft Word* cannot give a full WYSIWYG representation with a standard graphics display.

Chapter 10

Wraparound columns. Don't confuse side-by-side columns with the wraparound newspaper- or magazine-like column printing that's possible with another *Microsoft Word* option.

Wraparound columns represent an entirely different kind of printing. This option is available through the Format Division Layout menu. When that option is used, the paragraphs are automatically formatted for multicolumn printing. The text in the columns prints to the bottom of the page and is then wrapped to the top of the next column and printed down the page.

Two different methods. There are two different ways for *Microsoft Word* to align paragraphs side by side.

The first, and easiest, is to use a special style sheet that came with your program. The second way requires that you calculate the width and position of the side-by-side paragraphs. Then you have to type and format the paragraphs with indention commands.

The second method is much harder to use, but it'll give greater precision in controlling paragraph position. But the times you need that may be limited to producing camera-ready text with a laser printer.

Side-by-side the easy way. The easiest way to print paragraphs side by side is to attach the SIDEBY.STY style sheet to the document or division and use the style tags. Once this style sheet is attached to the document, you can use Alt commands to format the paragraphs for side-by-side printing. With those commands, you can swiftly align the paragraphs for two- or three-column side-by-side printing.

Using SIDEBY.STY. The SIDEBY.STY style sheet is calibrated for standard 8½-inch paper. If you are going to use 15-inch paper, you need to modify the style sheet. With this style sheet, you can set up two or three columns of equal width in a total text area 6 inches wide. The columns will be separated by a ½-inch gutter margin between them.

Formatting Paragraphs

Two-column side-by-side. Here is how to print two-column text:

- Type all the paragraphs normally, but in the order of the pairs or columns they are to be in. This will be either left-right-left-right, or left-center-right. Don't add extra space between paragraphs with carriage returns. If you need blank space, use the Space Before command from the Format Paragraph menu. 
  - Press the Esc key and type the letters *FSA*.
  - Press the F1 key and select SIDEBY.STY from the list. If you are running *Microsoft Word* from floppy disks, be sure to put the Utilities disk into a disk drive.
  - Press the Enter key. This attaches the style sheet to the document and makes the Alt commands active. 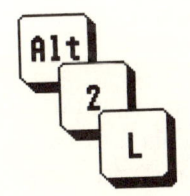
  - To format for the left column: Put the cursor anywhere on the paragraph; then hold down the Alt key and type 2L. 
  - To format for the right column: Put the cursor anywhere on the paragraph; then hold down the Alt key and type 2R.

  You don't have to put the paragraphs in pairs. You can align them left or right as you wish.

Three-column side-by-side. The directions above are for formatting two columns of side-by-side paragraphs. For formatting three-column side-by-side, substitute the commands Alt-3L, Alt-3C (for center column), and Alt-3R. All the other steps are the same.

Side-by-side the hard way. You may find using the SIDEBY.STY style sheet limiting. It predetermines the column widths and their positions on the page. There's another way to align paragraphs side-by-side that will give you precise control over the width of the columns and the place they'll be found

Chapter 10

on the printed page. This is a two-step process:

- Calculate the width and position of the paragraphs you want to print side by side.
- Type and format those paragraphs.

Calculating paragraph width and position. The paragraph width and position are set by assigning left and right indents to those paragraphs.

- Calculate the width of the area in which text will be printed. This will be the width of the paper, minus the left and right margins.
- Decide on the width of each paragraph to be printed side by side, and figure the amount of space you want in gutters between them.
- Calculate the indents that establish each paragraph's width and position.

Type and format the paragraphs. Here's how to format paragraphs for side-by-side printing:

- Type all the paragraphs one above the other in the normal style, in the order in which they are to appear. This will be either left-right-left-right or left-center-right. Don't add extra space between paragraphs with carriage returns. If you need blank space, use the Space Before command from the Format Paragraph menu.
- Put the cursor on the paragraph to be formatted side by side.
- Press the Esc key and type the letters *FS*.
- For a left-hand paragraph, type the indention measurement in the right-indent selection.
- For a right-hand paragraph, type the indention measurement for the left-indent selection.
- When formatting the first paragraph of a set, type a measurement into the Space Before field to indicate how many blank lines you want between sets.
- In the Side-by-Side selection, answer *Yes*.

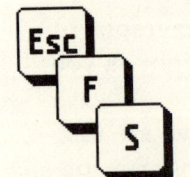

Two ways to streamline the process. Here is a quicker way:

- You can copy the paragraph formats and avoid having to go through all the steps for each paragraph. To learn how to do this, see Repeating Formatting and Copying Formatting.
- The format of any paragraph can be recorded as a style with the Format Style-Sheet Record command. After you format any paragraph, just record it as a style and then execute it with an Alt command.

Left indent controls where side-by-side paragraphs print. Your left-indent format controls the appearance of side-by-side paragraphs:

- If the left indent of a second paragraph is greater than the left indent for the paragraph preceding it, *Microsoft Word* will raise the second paragraph to print it beside the preceding one.
- If the left indent of a second paragraph is equal to the left indent for the paragraph preceding it, *Microsoft Word* will print the second one below the first.
- If the left indent of a second paragraph is less than the left indent for the paragraph, *Microsoft Word* will print the second paragraph below the longest paragraph in the group, and will print it at the indent specified for the second paragraph.
- If both right paragraphs have the same left indent, they'll align one under the other.

Chapter 11
Page Formatting and Divisions

Microsoft does not like to call a page a page. Instead, they confuse the issue by making arbitrary distinctions between pages and divisions. This chapter will try to explain this distinction so you won't be confused.

With *Microsoft Word*, page setup and layout is spread across several different areas, and you have to hunt around for them. One of the chief areas of page setup are the *Microsoft Word* divisions.

Divisions

A *division* is a section of a document in which all the pages have the same format. Because most documents have only one format throughout, they have only a single division. You can, however, set different parts of a document to have different page formats.

Basically, a division is a scheme where specific blocks of any text file may be marked off and each block is given its own special page formatting. All text then typed into that division will automatically format to that formatting. As you move the cursor from division to division, the default settings automatically change. In effect, one block can print under one set of rules and another block can print with a different set of rules.

Changing Page Formats in a Division

To change the page formatting for any division, all you have to do is use any of the format commands that control page formatting. These are:

- Format Division Margins
- Format Division Page-numbers

Chapter 11

- Format Division Layout
- Format Division line-Numbers
- Format Running-head

The division mark. The first use of any Format Division command will insert a division mark at the end of the document onscreen. A division mark is a double-dotted line all the way across the monitor screen. All of the page formatting codes are stored in the division mark. Every time you then use one of the Format Division commands, it'll update the information in the division mark.

A simple document has only one division in it. So it'll have consistent page-formatting throughout. But you can put additional division marks anyplace you need them and give each division between its own unique page formatting. The page formatting in the division mark controls the text above the division mark. While the cursor is in a division, all text typed will automatically conform to the format of the division.

You can copy any division mark to a glossary and then insert it any other else you want it. When you do so, all text above it to the next division mark will automatically assume its formatting.

The mark can be deleted from the document just like text. If you delete it, you'll lose all the special formatting in that division. If there's another division mark below that one, the text will assume its page formatting.

Controlling the Page Format

When you format pages with *Microsoft Word,* you control the following:

- Left, right, top, and bottom margins
- Paper size being used
- Number of columns of text
- Line numbers display and printing
- Page numbers and their location on the page
- Headers and footers (running heads)
- Footnotes and endnotes
- Total lines per page
- Lines actually printed

Page Formatting and Divisions

The default page settings. *Microsoft Word* comes from the factory preset for the following:

- Standard 8½ × 11 inch paper
- 1-inch top and bottom margins
- 1¼-inch left and right margins
- Arabic numbers for page numbering
- Page-number position is ½ inch from the top and 7¼ inches from the left

Changing the defaults. Whenever you change the setting of a Format Division option, while you are working on a plain document, then that new setting becomes the default setting for the default style sheet. *Microsoft Word* will remember the changes and will boot up the next time with those changes as the defaults.

The same is true for any style sheet you have attached to a document. Any changes you make with the Format Style-Sheet command become the default settings for that style sheet.

Division Format Commands and the Onscreen Display

Changing the setup with Format Division commands changes both the onscreen display and the resulting printed document. Within the limitations of the monitor and the video graphics card you're using, *Microsoft Word* will always display your documents as close to WYSIWYG as the system will allow.

To make sure your monitor displays your text as close as possible to the printed version, make sure that the Printer Display option is turned on. This feature is found on the command bar Options menu.

Controlling Page Size and Margins

Microsoft Word gives you full control over both page size and the margins used to print on the page. The page size is the actual size of paper you're using in the printer. The margins are the blank white borders around the printing on the page. By changing the margins, you can give your different kinds of documents just the look that gets the job done.

Chapter 11

Changing the page size. *Microsoft Word* comes preset to print on 8½ × 11 inch paper. If you change paper size, then you need to let the program know.

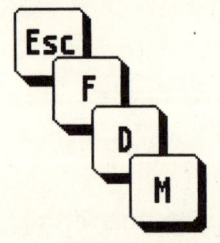

- Press the Esc key and type the letters *FDM*. Or use the command Alt-F4.
- In the selections page length and width, type the length and width of the different size paper in your printer.
- Press the Enter key.

Changing the margins. *Microsoft Word* comes preset to print with 1-inch top and bottom margins, and 1¼-inch left and right margins. Different kinds of documents work best with different margins.

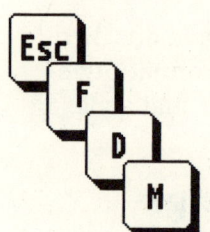

- Press the Esc key and type the letters *FDM*. Or use the command Alt-F4.
- Each of the margin settings can be set individually. Make them consistent if you want to have a balanced page. *Microsoft Word* measures margins from the corresponding edge of the printed page.
- Press the Enter key.

Using gutter margins. When you're writing documents that will be printed on back-to-back pages, you can set *Microsoft Word* to automatically insert extra space on the inside margin. This extra space is called a *gutter margin*. When you bind these documents, the gutter margin shifts the text toward the outer edge of the paper, thus making the document more attractive and easier to read.

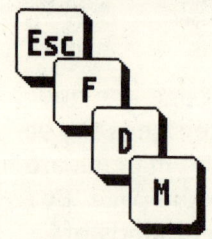

- Press the Esc key and type the letters *FDM*. Or use the command Alt-F4.
- In the gutter margin selection, type in the measurement for the extra space you want *Microsoft Word* to insert during printing. This will depend on how much space your binder will cover. But a common gutter is one-quarter-inch.
- Press the Enter key.

Page Formatting and Divisions

Printing smaller pages without changing paper size. There will be times when it is inconvenient to change paper size just to print smaller pages. If you're trying to print documents smaller than the standard 8½ × 11 inch paper, you may have a hard time finding continuous-feed paper smaller than that. Or you might have to use smaller paper and manually feed it into the printer one sheet at a time.

You can set the margins to print pages as if they appeared on smaller paper. One use for this is printing copy to be bound in smaller than standard-size paper. This works very well for camera-ready copy printed on a laser printer. Many books or user manuals use the standard 7 × 9 inch format. Just set your margins for 7 × 9 inch paper and repaginate your text file.

Formatting for Multiple Columns

Microsoft Word allows you to format pages to print text in multiple newspaper-style columns. There are two ways to print paragraphs in columns:

- Side-by-side
- Continuous

The side-by-side method is detailed in the chapter on formatting paragraphs.

Multiple-column pages. Through the Format Division Layout menu, you can easily set *Microsoft Word* to format your text file for multiple-column printing. The maximum number of columns that you can conveniently use depends on how wide the paper is, the width of the text to be printed in columns, and the size of the font you're printing.

Microsoft Word will automatically make all columns the same width and will place a half-inch gutter between the columns. You can change the gutter width on the same menu.

- Press the Esc key and type the letters *FDL*.
- Under Number of Columns, type the number of columns you want to use.
- If you want to change the space between columns, type in a different measurement.
- Press the Enter key.

Chapter 11

Displaying multicolumn formatting. *Microsoft Word* cannot display side-by-side columns on a standard display monitor. Documents formatted in multicolumn mode will display onscreen in a single column to the page break.

If you use the Print Repaginate command after multicolumn formatting, the column breaks will be marked by their column number at the left side of the text window.

If after repaginating to the multicolumn format, you switch to a different number of columns, the column break numbers will remain in the same place in the text.

If, after repaginating to the multicolumn format, you switch to single-column display, the former column-break numbers will be displayed as a single dotted line across the screen.

Controlling where column breaks fall. You can control the exact point where a column break will fall by inserting a column division-break. This is very useful for leaving room at the bottom of a column for pasting in an illustration. The column division is a double-dotted line that runs all the way across the screen.

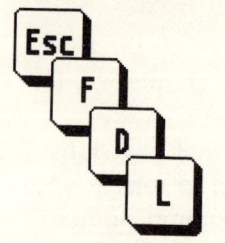

- Move the cursor highlight to the place where you want the column to break.
- Go to the Division Break option and select Column.
- Press the Esc key and type the letters *FDL*.
- Hold down the Ctrl key and press the Enter key.

At printing time, *Microsoft Word* will format the text to print down to the column-break point. At that point it'll break off printing and move the next text to the beginning of the next column.

You may find it convenient to turn on the line numbering display through the command bar Options menu. This will always tell you the line number the cursor is currently on. Use the Print Repaginate command to get a preview of where the column breaks will fall.

Page Formatting and Divisions

Banner heads over multicolumns. There is a very simple method for printing banner heads above text formatted in multicolumn. A banner heading stretches across all the columns. All you have to do is to format the text as a running head and then center-justify it.

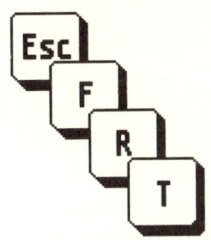

- Type the text for your banner head at the beginning of the multicolumn text.
- Put the cursor on the first character of the banner head.
- Press the Esc key and type the letters *FRT*. This will format the text as a running head. Make sure that the running head is set to print only on the first page. Turn off left- and right-page printing for the running head.
- Press the Enter key. 
- With the cursor still on the banner head, press the F10 key. 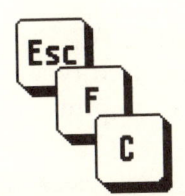
- Press the Esc key, type then letters *FC*; then select the format attributes and the font type and size you want the head to print in.
- Press the Enter key.

Banner text over multicolumns. It's possible to print banner text above text formatted in multicolumns. Banner text stretches across all the columns. Format the text as a running head; then adjust the top margin to allow room for the text as a running head and adjust the left and right indentions to make it fit the margins of your normal text printing area. This may take some measuring, some experimenting, and some trial printing to get it just right.

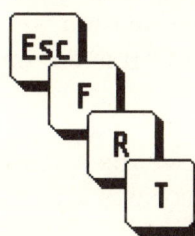

- Type the text for the banner head, banner text, and the text to be printed in multicolumn.
- Press the Esc key and type the letters *FRT*. This will format the text as a running head. Make sure that the running head is set to print only on the first page. Turn off left- and right-page printing for the running head.

105

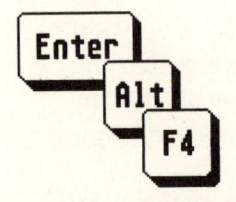

Chapter 11

- Press the Enter key.
- Hold down the Alt key and press the F4 key.
- Move the top margin down far enough leave enough room to print all the banner text. This is where you'll have to measure and experiment to learn how to get it right.
- Expand the cursor highlight to cover the banner text.
- Press the Esc key and type the letters *FP*. 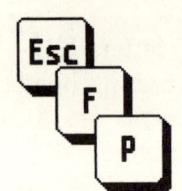
- Adjust the left and right indents until the banner text fits on the page as you want it. And justify it to match the justification of the multicolumn text. 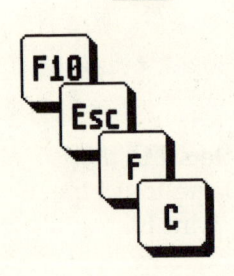
- If you want your a banner head to be distinctive from the banner text, put the cursor on the banner head and press the F10 key.
- Press the Esc key, type then letters *FC*, then select the format attributes, font type, and size that you want the head to print in. Be sure to center-justify it.
- Press the Enter key.

Using Multiple-Page Formats

When you want to use multiple-page formats in a single document, start a new division where you need it and tell *Microsoft Word* where the new page formats begin. You start a new division by inserting a division mark.

Inserting a division mark. Here are the steps for inserting a division mark:

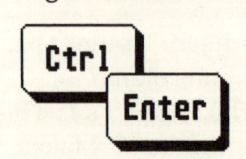

- Put the cursor on the first character of the line you want to start a new division.
- Hold down the Ctrl key and press the Enter key.

Microsoft Word will insert a division mark above the cursor to set the end of the previous division. If the cursor was on the end mark, it will shift below the new division.

Page Formatting and Divisions

Formatting a new division. When you start any new division you need to set up the new page format for that division so it will print as you want it.

- Put the cursor in the new division to be formatted.
- Use each of the major options on the Format Division menu to set up the Margins, Page Numbers, Layout, and Line Numbers as you want them for the new division.

Controlling where the new page format begins. When you insert a division mark, the default setting will cause the text below it to print on the next page unless you select a division break other than Page in the Format Division Layout menu.

Printing Page Numbers in Documents

Microsoft Word gives you three different ways to print numbers in your documents. You can:

- Simply turn on normal page numbering, and set it up as you want it. This will print the page numbers at the same position on each page. Default page numbering puts the numbers at the top-right corner of each printed page. The numbers will be ½ an inch down from the top and 7¼ inches from the left edge. Standard page numbering also offers several options for varying the printing.
- Print the page numbers as a header through the Running Head option on the main format menu. This will print the page numbers at the bottom of the page at any position you want them. You can even print side-to-side numbers for even/odd page numbering.
- Print the page numbers as a footer through the Running Head option on the main format menu. This will print the page numbers at the top of the page at any position you want them. You can even print side-to-side numbers for even/odd page numbering.

With any of these three methods, you can number the document continuously or start page numbering over at each division break.

Chapter 11

Standard page numbering. Using the default page numbering is as as easy as turning it on. It's available through the Format Division menu under Page Numbers. Default page numbering puts the numbers at the top right of each printed page. The numbers will be ½ an inch down from the top and 7¼ inches from the left edge.

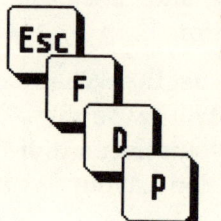

- Press the Esc key and type the letters *FDP*.
- Answer *Yes*, select Continuous, and make sure the number format is on 1.
- Press the Enter key. Page numbering is turned on.

If standard numbering won't work with the above steps, try telling it to start printing at page 1, even if you have it set for continuous printing. Some printers have to be told.

Numbers at left, center, or right. Once you set page numbering, the numbers will print at the same position on every page throughout the document. But you can position the numbers anywhere left, right, or center by varying the measurement from the left edge of the paper. If you print documents on different-sized papers, you'll need to adjust this measurement accordingly.

Numbers at either top or bottom. Page numbers can be printed in either the top or bottom margins. For standard 8½ × 11 inch paper, set it to print 10 inches down from the top.

If you set distance from the top so that it falls in the body of the document (between the top and bottom margins), the page number may not print, depending on the printer you're using.

The only way to have page numbering in the same margin as a a Running Head is to make that numbering a part of the header or footer.

Starting page numbering over in each division. Page numbering may be started over again at the beginning of each division. This requires using the Format Division Page-numbers command in each division where page numbering is to start over again. Just change numbering from Continuous to Start and tell *Microsoft Word* with what page number and format to begin printing.

This is useful when printing large documents with chapters or major parts and you need to start numbering at the beginning of each of those chapters or parts. See also the topic below.

Different numbering formats. *Microsoft Word* lets you use one of five different numbering formats to number the pages. And you can change numbering formats in each division, if you also tell it to restart page numbering at the beginning of each division. These five numbering formats are:

- Arabic
- Uppercase Roman numerals
- Lowercase Roman numerals
- Uppercase alphabetic
- Lowercase alphabetic

It's common to number the front matter pages of a book (the table of contents, preface, and foreword) in lowercase Roman numerals, then switch to Arabic numerals for the body of the document, then switch back to Roman numerals for the pages of appendices and the index.

Page numbering as a header or footer. The most flexible way to number pages is to put them in either a header or a footer. *Microsoft Word* calls both of these *Running Heads.* Page numbering as a header or footer is covered in the chapter on headers and footers.

The Format Division Layout Menu

With one exception, the features on the Format Division Layout menu control options that are used with the general page layout procedures detailed earlier in this chapter. That exception is the footnote/endnote–positioning toggle that is the first option on the menu. This toggle selects between placing footnotes on the same page as the reference and placing endnotes at the end of the division.

Number of columns. This option lets you set the the number of columns in which *Microsoft Word* will automatically print the text you type. Standard text is single-column. If you

Chapter 11

select multiple columns, the text formats into columns of equal width, with the same distance or gutter space between the columns. This produces newspaper- or magazine-like printing.

Space between columns. In the printing trade, the space between columns is called the *gutter space* or simply a *gutter*. Don't confuse this with gutter margins described earlier in this chapter. The default space or gutter between columns is half an inch no matter how many columns you choose. Obviously, the more columns you select, the more space is eaten up by the gutters. So you can make more room for printing by narrowing the gutters. Change the space to whatever you like or whatever works best for your particular needs. Use any of the measurement standards that *Microsoft Word* recognizes: inches, centimeters, P10, P12, or lines. It will automatically convert to the standard that the program is currently set to use.

You can also widen the gutters for artistic or layout purposes. If, for example, you intend to put an illustration down the center of the page, you can widen the gutter to make room for it. If this narrows the column width too much, widen the left and right margins to compensate.

The type of division break. There are five different types of division breaks. These determine where and how the new page format begins and where the new page starts printing. When you insert a division mark, the default setting will cause the text below it to print on the next page unless you select a division break other than Page in the Format Division Layout menu.

There are five optional division breaks you can use to tell *Microsoft Word* how to print the text within the division. Table 11-1 is a list of these division-break options with descriptions of their effect on printing.

Table 11-1. Division-Break Options

Command	Effect
Page	This is the default setting for *Microsoft Word*. *Microsoft Word* will break the page at the division mark. The page formatting for the next division will begin printing on the new page.
Continuous	This new formatting will begin on the next page, but *Microsoft Word* will finish printing the current page in the old format. If necessary,

Page Formatting and Divisions

Command	Effect
	it'll use text from the new division to fill the page. If you don't want it to use text from the following division, add enough blank lines with carriage returns to fill out the bottom of the page.
Column	This will break a column of text at the division mark. *Microsoft Word* will begin printing the text below it in the next column.
Even	This breaks the page at the division mark. The text below the division mark will begin printing on the next even-numbered page. This will leave a blank page if the last page of the previous division was even-numbered.
Odd	This breaks the page at the division mark. The text below the division mark will begin printing on the next odd-numbered page. This will leave a blank page if the last page of the previous division was odd-numbered. The most common use of this division break is to begin new chapters always on odd-numbered pages.

Printing Line Numbers in Documents

Usually it doesn't matter what specific line anything is printed on. But *Microsoft Word* has a feature that will print Arabic line numbers in the left margin of any document. The body text will print in its formatted position, and the numbers will print in the left margin.

This is the most commonly used in the legal profession, for preparing legal briefs, or contracts. It's sometimes used in screenplays, teleplays, stageplays, and shooting scripts. The option is useful whenever you must be able to refer quickly to specific lines on a page.

This option is available through the Format Division line-Numbers menu.

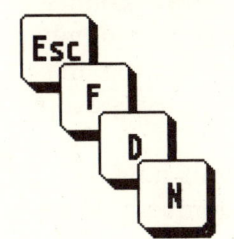

- Press the Esc key and type the letters *FDN*.
- Answer *Yes* to turn it on; *No* to turn it off.
- Change any of the other options on the menu.
- Press the Enter key.

Restart line numbering. You can add line numbers to to an entire document or to selected parts of the document. There are three options for where the line numbers restart, as shown in Table 11-2.

Chapter 11

Table 11-2. Page-Numbering Options

Option	Effect
Page	This is the default setting. It will start the line numbering over again at the beginning of each printed page.
Division	This will will ignore standard page breaks and print line numbers consecutively to each division break. Line numbers restart after each division break.
Continuous	This will ignore page and division breaks and will print line numbers consecutively from the beginning to the end of the document.

Beginning and ending line numbers in the document. You can begin line numbering anywhere you want in the document and can continue with them until the end of the document. Do this by placing a division mark above the portion to be line-numbered. Then turn on Line Numbering and set the Restart option at to Continuous.

You can begin line numbering anywhere you want in the document and then turn it off at the point where you don't need it. This is done by placing a division mark at the beginning and the end of the portion to be line-numbered. Turn on line numbering only within that division, and set the option restart at to Division.

Some guidelines and examples. The above method can be used to turn on line numbering in specific divisions. If you skip divisions, numbering will pick up in the next division where the last division left off.

If you use Print Selection to print a portion from a text file, the line numbering will begin with 1 on the first line of the selection. There are some things to consider when printing a selection or specific pages: The print routine always counts pages from the beginning of the text file, and the page number printed will be the actual page of the document. But the line numbering will begin with 1 on the first page of the hardcopy that's printed.

Controlling distance from text. This controls how far from the body text you want to print the line numbers. The default distance is .4 inch. When printing line numbers, the body text will print in its formatted position and the numbers will print in the left margin.

Page Formatting and Divisions

You may place the line numbers almost anywhere in the left margin, as long as you set them slightly less than the full margin width. You may use any of the measurement standards that *Microsoft Word* recognizes: inches, centimeters, P10, P12, or lines. They'll be converted automatically to whatever measurements you're currently using.

If you use gutter margins with documents to be bound, the line-number distance from the body text will not change.

Increments. You don't have to print the number of every line in a page, division, or document. Sometimes that's just too much. You can set the increments by line and can print only every second, third, or fourth line, and so on. The most commonly used increments are 1, 5, and 10.

Displaying line numbers. Line numbers won't display onscreen. To keep track of the position of the line numbers, call the command bar Options and turn on the line numbers option there. This will indicate line number position on the status line between page and column numbers.

Some basic guidelines. Here are the rules governing line-counting.

- Only the lines in the body text are counted. Lines in headers and footers are ignored.
- Even lines with only a carriage return on them are counted and numbered. If you use double, triple, or larger line spacing, the spaces between lines are ignored. Space added between paragraphs with Space After and Space Before is ignored.
- When printing side-by-side columns, line numbers will only be printed to the left of each horizontal line regardless of the number of columns.
- When printing in multicolumn format (the newspaper-like columns), line numbers will print to the left of every column. There will be a number for every line in the columns.
- If there isn't enough room for the whole number in the left margin or in the gutters between columns, the number will be truncated to the most significant digits that will fit in the space. For example, if you're printing two-column with default settings, there's room for only a single digit to print. So

113

Chapter 11

on line 54, for instance, the first digit will be omitted and only the 4 will print.
- You can make room for more digits to print in the left margin or in the gutters between columns by widening the left margin or space between columns. The left margin is set up in the Format Division Margins menu. The space between columns is set up in the Format Division Layout menu.
- You can also make more room by simply decreasing the distance between the numbers and the body text. The default is .4 inch. Try adjusting that to 1 li (line) or .17 inch.

Chapter 12
Setting and Using Tabs

If you know how to type, you know what tab stops are. *Tab stops* are preset positions across the page to which the carriage (or cursor) can be quickly moved when you press the tab key. With a word processing program like *Microsoft Word*, you have much more control over the tab stops. You can even set up special-purpose tabs that have automatic features.

Most people use tabs to hang indented lines of typed text. With *Microsoft Word,* this type of formatting is done with indention commands. Those are controlled through the Format Paragraph menu.

In word processing, tabs are usually used to indent the first line of a paragraph and to type numbered lists of information. You can do that, or you can use the Format Paragraph menu indentions.

Tabs are best used for typing tables of information. With tabs, you can quickly align columns of information in the tables as you wish them to be. If the preset tabs aren't satisfactory, you can customize the tab settings for any paragraph.

A paragraph will always have the default tab settings every half inch, unless you assign that paragraph custom tab settings. Adding even one custom tab to a paragraph automatically clears all the default tabs from that paragraph.

With most word processing programs, once you set the tab stops, they're in effect for the rest of the document. With *Microsoft Word,* you can customize tab-stop settings for each paragraph in the document. You don't have to go through the setup procedure every time. Because the tab settings are part of the paragraph formatting, you can copy that formatting to other paragraphs.

Most word processors only allow you a single measurement standard for tab stops, usually in 12 point. Often, if you're allowed more than one measurement standard, they'll be 10 and 12 point. And you may not be able to use both in

Chapter 12

the same document. As a result, a tab is set at a simple column position across the line of type.

With *Microsoft Word,* you can set tab stops precisely where you want them. Default measurements are made in inches. So if you want a tab set at 1.55 inches or 2.33 inches, it will print exactly there. But you can also use centimeters, 10p, 12p, and lines, depending on the particular standard needed for that particular document.

You can use any or all of these measurements at once in the same paragraph or table. If you have *Microsoft Word* set for one measurement standard, and you type in a tab setting in one of the other four standards, it will be converted by the program and the tab will be set exactly in the spot you want it.

Microsoft Word comes with tab stops preset every half an inch, up to the six-inch mark on the ruler line. These are all normal, left-aligned tab stops. If you change the measurement standard from inches to one of the other measurements, the tab distance will remain the same.

Typewriters, and many word processor, only permit left-justified table columns. *Microsoft Word* allows you to vary the alignment of each tab setting. Along with left-justified tabs, you have center justification, right justification, or decimal justification. You can also set a tab that automatically draws a vertical line at a tab stop.

Setting Up and Using Tab Stops

This section contains general information for setting up all types of tabs. It includes many tips for using tab stops in your documents.

Turning on the ruler line. Before you start working with tabs, the first thing you need to do is turn on the ruler line so you can see what you're doing. The ruler line is turned on through the Window Options menu.

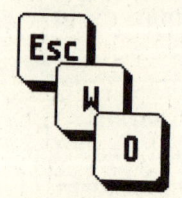

- Press the Esc key and type the letters *WO*.
- Under the Ruler option, answer *Yes*.
- Press the Enter key.

116

Setting and Using Tabs

If you leave *Microsoft Word* with the exit command (rather than by turning off the computer) it will save this change as the default. The ruler line will be visible when you boot up the program.

Changing the default tab settings. *Microsoft Word* comes with default tab stops set every half-inch across the ruler line to the six-inch mark. You can change the default tab distance through the command bar Options menu.

These default tabs are all normal, left-aligned tab stops. You can't change that. They're set with inches as the measurement standard. If you change from inches to another standard, *Microsoft Word* will convert your setting to that standard. The actual tab distance will remain the same.

If you find you always use custom tabs instead of default tabs, save your tab formatting to a glossary and copy it into your documents from there.

- Press the Esc key and type the letter O.
- Under default tab width, type in the measurement you want for your default tabs. You can use any one of the five measurement standards.
- Press the Enter key.

This will change the default tab width for the duration of the work session. Those tabs will be applied to every paragraph in any document you write during that period. If you want to leave without making this a permanent default, just turn off the computer to exit at the end of your work session. The changes won't become permanent until you use the Quit command to leave *Microsoft Word*.

Setting a tab stop. To set a tab on a typewriter, you use the space bar to move to the place you want a tab and then press the Set Tab key. With *Microsoft Word*, you use the Format Tab Set menu and tell it the column number on which you want the tab to be set.

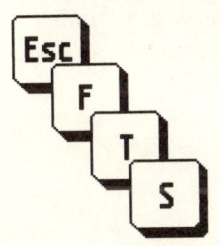

- Press the Esc key and type the letters *FTS*.
- Type the number value for the position of the new tab. The default measurement is in inches. If you enter any other measurement, it'll be converted. If you use lines (li) as a measurement for this, it will be a column setting.

117

Chapter 12

- Change the tab alignment and leader character, if you wish.
- Press the Enter key.

The tabs always begin at the left margin and move to the right across the ruler line. But you don't have to set them in that order.

Custom tab stops are set for each paragraph, and each line in a table must be a separate paragraph. So make sure to put the highlight on the paragraph mark before you issue a carriage return. The new paragraph will have the same tab formatting as the last.

Speed-setting custom tab. There's a speed command you can use to go right to the Format Tab Set menu to set the tabs directly on the ruler line.

- Hold down the Alt key and press the F1 key. The Format Tab Set menu will appear.
- Notice the highlight that appears on the ruler line.
- Use the right- and left-arrow keys to move to the position you need to insert a tab. The cursor position is indicated in the highlight on the menu.
- If you need to change the alignment or the leader character, press the tab key. This will restore the normal function of the arrow keys, the highlight will leave the ruler line, and you can set the alignment and/or leader character options.
- Press the Ins key.
- To add another tab, press the F1 key. The highlight will return to the ruler line. Repeat the steps above.
- When finished adding tabs, press the Enter key.

Clearing a tab stop. You can clear any tab stop that has been set with the Format Tab Clear command.

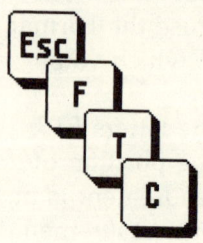

- Press the Esc key and type the letters *FTC*.
- Type the measurement location for the tab to be cleared. If deleting more than one tab, type in all their locations. Separate them with commas and don't leave blank spaces.
- Press the Enter key.

118

Setting and Using Tabs

Speed-deleting custom tabs. There's a speed command you can use to go right to the Format Tab Set menu to delete the tabs directly from the ruler line.

- Hold down the Alt key and press the F1 key. The Format Tab Set menu will appear.
- Notice the highlight that appears on the ruler line.
- Use the right- and left-arrow keys to move to the custom tab you want to delete.
- Press the Del key.
- To delete another custom tab, repeat the steps above.
- When you've finished deleting custom tabs, press the Enter key.

Setting left tabs with the mouse. If you have a mouse installed, there's a speedy way to set left-justified tabs and to move them left or right.

- Hold down the Alt key and press the F1 key. The Format Tab Set menu will appear.
- Notice the highlight that appears on the ruler line.
- Put the mouse pointer at the exact spot on the ruler line you wish to set the tab.
- Click the Left Button.

Moving left tabs with the mouse. If you have a mouse installed, there's a speedy way to move left-justified tabs left or right on the ruler line.

- Hold down the Alt key and press the F1 key. The Format Tab Set menu will appear.
- Notice the highlight that appears on the ruler line.
- Put the mouse pointer on the tab to be moved.
- Press the left mouse button and drag the *L* to the new location.
- Release the mouse button.

Reset all tabs to defaults. You can quickly remove all custom tabs from a paragraph and restore the default tab settings.

Chapter 12

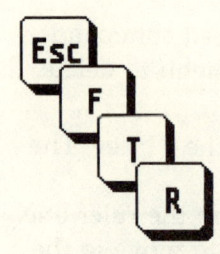

- Put the cursor in the paragraph where you wish to remove all custom tab stops.
- Press the Esc key and type the letters *FTR*.

Different kinds of tabs. The different kinds of tab stops you can set within a paragraph are named according to their special alignment on the page. They are:

- Left
- Right
- Center
- Decimal
- Vertical

Left-aligned. This is the default setting. As you type the text at this tab stop, it'll be left-justified.

Right-aligned. As you type the text at this tab stop, it'll be right-justified.

Center-aligned. As you type the text at this tab stop, it'll be center-justified.

Decimal tabs. As you type text at a decimal tab, it'll insert left until you type the decimal in the number. Then the text will begin inserting to the right. This is for listing numbers in a column and having the decimals stack up vertically. If the entry has no decimal in it, the text will be right-justified.

Vertical tab. This automatically will draw a vertical line at the tab position. It will extend downward through every line of the table.

Displaying tab type. The type of tab will be displayed on the ruler line when you set it. See Table 12-1.

Table 12-1. Tab Identifiers on Ruler Line

Symbol	Tab Type
L	Left-aligned tab.
R	Right-aligned tab.
C	Center-aligned tab.
D	Decimal-aligned tab.
I	Vertical-line tab.

Leader characters. Leader characters are symbols you can assign to a tab. When you type the text at that stop, and then tab to the next stop, *Microsoft Word* will automatically insert the leader characters to that next tab stop. So it "leads" you to the text at the next tab setting.

Blank. This is the default setting. If you leave the setting blank, the unused space will be left blank.

Dots. If you select dots as the leader character, the unused space will have dots printed in it up to the next tab setting. Dots are often used as leader characters in a table of contents. This results in a line of dots leading from the end of the chapter name to the page number.

Underscore marks. This is the same as the underlining key on the keyboard. If you select underscore marks as the leader character, the unused space will be have underlining printed in it up to the next tab stop.

Hyphens. If you select hyphens as the leader character, the unused space will be filled with hyphens to the next tab stop.

121

Chapter 13
Making Tables of Information

The purpose of a table is to arrange your information by category in neat rows and columns. Tables compile your data and information for easy reference. They highlight special information by making it visually distinct from the rest of the body text. Tab stops control column placement and the type of alignment each category is given.

Making a Table
If the table heading is to be justified differently, or printed with different indention or character formatting, then it needs to be in a paragraph of its own.

The body of a table is created by first setting a custom tab-stop for each column in the table. At that time, you can set the alignment or justification of the text in each column. You can also insert vertical lines as tabs between the columns. Finally, type the table using those tabs.

If you use many tables in your documents, you can save time by storing the table on disk as a block when it's tabulated the way you want it. You won't have to go to the trouble of typing similar tables later on. Instead, you can use the Transfer Merge command to copy it into the document where needed.

Over time, you'll assemble an archive of tables ready for use. If you have to type a table similar to one in the archive, just copy it from the archive and edit it.

Even if nothing is similar but the tab settings, it'll still save time. Copy it into your new document, delete the unnecessary text, and use the already set tabs. This is especially useful if you're using larger or smaller or proportionally spaced fonts in the tables.

123

Chapter 13

Left-justified columns. Most table columns use left-aligned tabs. When you type text or numbers into a left-justified tab, it inserts from left to right, in normal typing fashion. This keeps the text lined up neatly on the left side of the columns and is sufficient for most purposes. Left-justified tabs were all you could use with a typewriter. The habit lingers into word processing. Printers have long used other types of alignments in printing books, magazines, and newspapers. Their typesetting equipment have made the following formats commonplace.

Right-justified and decimal columns. These two are discussed together because they are usually used for the same type of information, and a decimal tab is essentially an enhancement of right-justified tab. When putting numbers in a table column, right-justified and decimal tabs get the job done quickly.

When you type numbers at a right-justified tab, they insert from right to left. This is important, because it keeps the numbers and commas stacked in the best possible way for easy reading.

When expressing numbers that have decimal values appended, decimal tabs can serve you better than right-justified tabs. The decimal part of a number may vary from zero to many decimal places. A right-justified column of numbers with different-length decimal parts would be virtually unreadable.

Decimal tabs do essentially the same thing as right-justified tabs, but they give you the additional element of aligning numbers at their decimal points. When you type numbers at a decimal tab, they insert from right to left until you type the decimal, and then the numbers insert left to right at the tab stop. This keeps decimal numbers aligned for the easiest possible reading.

Center-justified columns. The least used tabs for table columns are center-justified. Center justification leaves ragged right and left margins inside the columns, so it defeats one of the main reasons for putting text into tables. Columns of numbers can become especially difficult to read if center-justified.

Making Tables of Information

You can use center justification to give some information its own special look. For example, if your table contains one-word responses like *yes, no, up, down, left, right, n/a,* a single digit, or some other brief entry, you can make the column more attractive by centering those responses.

Typing the table as a single paragraph. With *Microsoft Word,* you can type a table as a single paragraph. This only works if you intend to use the same tabs throughout the table. When a table is typed as a single paragraph, any change you make to tab stops or indentions will be effective throughout the entire table. All the columns and rows will immediately shift to reflect the changes.

If the table heading is to be justified differently, or printed with different indention or character formatting, it needs to be in a paragraph of its own.

To type a table as a single paragraph:

- Type the first line of the table using the tabs.
- At the end of the last entry, use the command Shift-Enter. (Hold down the Shift key and then press the Enter key.) This adds a new, blank line to the paragraph without adding a carriage return. (It will display onscreen as a downward-pointing arrow.)
- Type each line of the table, repeating the previous step, until you have completed the table.
- Press the Enter key.

You have just typed a table as a single paragraph. If you later need to add further lines to the table, use the Shift-Enter command to add blank lines to the table. The tabs are part of the paragraph format so you can still use them.

Tables Typed in 12-Point, Fixed-Space Fonts

The steps used to set up and type a table depend specifically on the type and size of the font in which the table will be printed. This section contains the instructions for the most common type of table you're likely to type and print. See the following two sections if this one does not cover your needs.

Chapter 13

With the standard monochrome or color display, *Microsoft Word* displays the equivalent of a 12-point, fixed-space font. So if you're planning to print in that font, the screen accurately reflects the table to be printed.

Making the 12-point table. Here are the steps necessary to make a 12-point table:

- Move the cursor to the line on which the table is to begin. (If the table heading is to be justified differently or printed with different indention or character formatting, it needs to be in a paragraph of its own.)
- Use Alt-F1 to call the Format Tabs Set menu. Set every tab where you need it to be. If you don't have the ruler line turned on, then toggle it with the command bar Options menu. You'll need it to see what you're doing.
- Type the text for the first table column.
- Press the Tab key to move to the next column, and type what goes there. Repeat this process for every column in the table.
- At the end of every line, use Shift-Enter to add a line to the paragraph without a carriage return.
- When you reach the end of the last line in the table, press the Enter key.

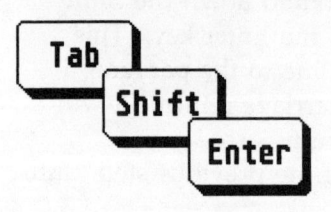

Multiple paragraphs in a table. The above directions will produce a table typed as a single paragraph. Every tab throughout the table will be consistent. If you need to change tab settings in the middle of a table, you'll need to start a new paragraph and set the tabs for it.

You can have every line in a table set up as a paragraph with its own custom tab settings. Use the Enter key to issue carriage returns for every line of the table. Then go back and set the custom tabs as you need them.

If you want every line of a table to be a paragraph, but want the same tabs for each line:

- Issue a carriage return to start the first paragraph of the table.

Making Tables of Information

- Use Alt-F1 to call the Format Tabs Set menu. Set every tab where it should be.
- Put the cursor on the paragraph mark at the end of the paragraph.
- Press the Enter key once for each line in the table.
- Go back to the first line of the table. Type each line of the table with the tabbed columns. But at the end of each line, use the left- or down-arrow key to move to the next line.

If you can't see the paragraph mark at the end of the paragraph, then you have Options Visible set to None. Call the main Options menu and set this to either Partial or Complete in order to see the return marks at the end of paragraphs.

Repositioning columns. Sometimes you really don't see how well you've spaced the columns in a table until you print a hardcopy. Or you may need to insert or delete a column item from that table, and there isn't room with the current settings. No problem. Once you have typed a table, the columns in it can always be repositioned simply by moving the tab stops.

- Use Alt-F1 to call the Format Tabs Set menu.
- Use the up- and down-arrow keys to move the highlight to the tab you want to move.
- Press the Del key and delete it.
- Use the left- and right-arrow keys to move the highlight to the new position for the tab. Don't move the highlight past an existing tab stop. That would swap the positions of the tab stops and throw your columns out of alignment.
- Press the Insert key.

Microsoft Word will shift the data in the column to the new tab-stop position.

Repositioning left-aligned columns with the mouse. There is a fast way to reposition left-justified tabs with the mouse. This will only work with left-justified tab settings. If you try moving any other type of tab with the mouse, *Microsoft Word* will convert that tab to a left-justified tab.

Chapter 13

- Use Alt-F1 to call the Format Tabs Set menu.
- Put the mouse pointer on the left-justified tab you want to move.
- Press the left mouse button and drag the L to the new position.
- Release the mouse button.

Speed-setting tabs with the mouse. There is a fast way to set left-justified tabs with the mouse. This can also be used to change the alignment of a previously set tab of any type to a left-justified tab.

- Use Alt-F1 to call the Format Tabs Set menu.
- Put the mouse pointer at the position on the ruler line where you want to place a left-justified tab.
- Click the left button on the mouse.
- To change the alignment of any tab set this way, use the up- and down-arrow keys to move to the tab to be changed. Then press the Tab key to escape from this macro, and use the space bar to move to the alignment category you want.
- Press the Enter key.

Tables Printed with Different-Sized Fonts

With the standard monochrome or color display, *Microsoft Word* displays the equivalent of a 12-point, fixed-space font. If you're going to print the table in a different font, the screen will not reflect what will be printed. You must set up the table to print the way you want it, regardless of its onscreen alignment.

The steps for setting up and typing a table depend on the type and size of the font in which you are going to print the table. This section contains the instructions for setting up and typing tables that are to be printed in a font size different from the default.

This means:

- First you must type the table using *Microsoft Word's* default tab settings.
- Go back and set up custom tabs that will align the entire table on the page as you want it to print.

Making Tables of Information

- Larger fonts take up more space on the page. You may have to narrow the paragraph margins and/or shift the indentions to keep a table centered on the page. Tables are rarely printed in a larger font than the normal body text.
- Smaller fonts take up less space on the page. So you'll have to widen the paragraph margins and/or indents to keep a table centered on the page. It's far more common to print tables in a smaller than a larger font.

Typing a table with a different-sized font. Before you begin, turn on the ruler line, set command bar Options Visible to Partial, and turn on the style bar. With the style bar turned on, an asterisk will display at the beginning of any default-formatted paragraph.

The steps in this subsection will result in a table typed as a single paragraph:

1. Put the cursor on the paragraph mark where the table is to begin.
2. Press the Esc key and type the letters *FC* to call the Format Character menu.
3. Select the font attributes, type, and size; then press the Enter key.
4. Type the text for the first column. The text will insert formatted for the type, size, and attributes you have selected.
5. Then press the Tab key and type the next column. Repeat this for every column in the table.
6. At the end of the first line, use Shift-Enter to add a line without a carriage return.
7. Repeat steps 4–6 for every line in the table except the last.
8. At the end of the last line in the table, press the Enter key.

Setting the tab stops. Get out some scratch paper and use it to make your computations for this stage of the setup.

- Count the number of characters in the widest entry in each column.
- Convert the numbers to decimal inches by dividing the number of characters by the font size. (It's measured in characters per inch.)

129

Chapter 13

- Make up your mind how much space you want to leave between the columns and add it to the decimal inches.
  - Use Alt-F1 to call the Format Tabs Set menu.
  - Use the left- and right-arrow keys to move the highlight to the place you wish to put the first custom tab. Then press the Insert key.
- Repeat the previous step for every custom tab you wish to set.
- When finished, press the Enter key.
- The tabs are all left-justified. If you wish to use a different alignment, change each tab stop accordingly.
- Test print the page with the table on it to see how it looks. If it isn't positioned properly on the page, adjust the left or right indention until it's correct.

Tables Printed with Proportionally Spaced Fonts

This section contains the instructions for setting up and typing tables that are to be printed in proportionally spaced type, in any size font.

Proportionally spaced fonts can cause annoying problems when you're trying to determine measurements for placing text on the page. Setting up a table printed in proportional spacing depends not only on the size of the font but on the individual characters typed into the columns. So if you're going to work with them, you need to understand what they are.

Proportionally spaced fonts are distinguished by the fact that they vary the distance allotted to each character according to the width of the character. In ordinary fonts, the *i* and the *w* are given equal space on the page, although the *i* may look slightly isolated and the *w* a little cramped. Proportionally spaced type would move the other letters closer to the *i* and spread them out to give the *w* more room. When the text is printed, the characters are just far enough apart to keep them separate and distinct. For this reason, the length of a line must be determined by the sum of its proportional widths instead of by simply counting the number of characters in the line.

Making Tables of Information

With the standard monochrome or color display, *Microsoft Word* displays the equivalent of a 12-point, fixed-space font. What you see onscreen in no way reflects how proportionally spaced text will print. Lines with the same number of characters will display the same length onscreen. But when they print, their appearance may be radically altered. The printer will adjust the spacing between the letters and words.

Setting up for proportional spacing. If you're going to print the table in a proportionally spaced font, what you see onscreen cannot be trusted. You must set up the table to print properly on paper, and pay little regard to its appearance onscreen.

This means:

- Type the table using *Microsoft Word's* default tab settings.
- Set up custom tabs that will align the columns in the table according to their actual width when printed.
- Bigger characters use more space than skinny characters.
- Larger fonts will take up more space when printed than they appear to take onscreen. Don't try to line up column entries by adding or deleting blank spaces. You must always use tabs to fix the columns and keep the text where you want it.
- Smaller fonts take up less space than they appear to take onscreen, so you will have to widen the paragraph margins and/or indentions to keep a table centered on the page. It's more common to print tables in a smaller than in a larger font.

Editing and Reorganizing a Table

Once you have a table set up and typed, it's easy to edit and reorganize it. In fact, it's very similar to editing and formatting any other text. You have to remember that you are dealing with lines and columns of text rather than sentences and paragraphs.

- You can delete, copy, and move a line just as you would in a normal paragraph.
- You can format the characters in a table just like any other text. The only exceptions come when you attempt formatting that contradicts the tab settings.

Chapter 13

- You can turn on the column selection mode and then delete, copy, and move a column to rearrange the table.
- You can select a column and use it as a sort key to rank all the rows in a table.
- You can select a column in a heading and perform calculations on the figures in it.

Guidelines for cutting and pasting and copying columns. If your table has many columns, and different kinds of tab alignments, cut-and-paste can lead you into some tricky problems. It's a good idea to copy the entire table to a file of its own before you start revising it. Then you can delete your errors and merge the untouched copy back into your document.

It's relatively easy to cut and paste within a standard three- to five-column table and to copy columns from a table.

Cutting is simple: Highlight the section to be cut and press the Del key. When it's deleted, it goes to the scrap. You can then insert it anywhere by moving the cursor and pressing the Ins key. Copying just means marking it with the highlight and using the Copy command to send it to a glossary or a file of its own.

When you mark the column for these functions, be sure to include the column's trailing tab characters under the highlight. To see them, you must have the command bar Options Visible display set to Complete. They will be the small, right-arrow symbols that appear just after the last text in a column entry. If you don't get them all, you'll ruin the alignment of the column you're deleting, copying, or inserting.

When you delete or insert columns (and trailing tab characters), the columns to the right of the affected column will be shifted to accomodate the insertion or deletion. In the scrap display (on the status line), you'll see small boxes. Those boxes represent the end of a row in the column. This is also a reminder that the scrap holds a column instead of ordinary text.

When you widen a table by cutting and pasting columns, be sure to leave enough room on the right margin for the insertion. And the space into which you are inserting the column must have at least as many lines as what you are inserting. If

Making Tables of Information

this isn't so, you can wind up with word-wrapped columns, and that can ruin the appearance of the entire table. To correct this, adjust the left and right indentions until the rows and columns match. You may even have to do some character deletion and retyping.

If the column headings are in the same paragraph as the column text, then you can cut and paste the heading and column together. Usually, a column head will have different formatting, and thus be in a separate paragraph. In that event, you will have to cut and paste them separately.

The last column in a table requires some special handling. This is covered in a subsection of its own.

How to select columns. This subsection will cover use of the column-selection mode. It is toggled on or off with the command Shift-F6. You need to be sure to turn it off before returning to write-and-edit mode.

Before you begin, turn on the ruler line, set command bar Options Visible to Partial, and turn on the style bar. All of these will help you to see what you are doing. You know what the ruler line is. The Options Visible setting will let you see the paragraph marks at the end of paragraphs. With the style bar turned on, an asterisk will display at the beginning of any default-formatted paragraph.

- Put the cursor on the first character of the column you want to highlight.

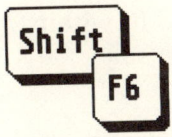

- Hold down the Shift key and press the F6 key. This turns on the column-select mode. (You can tell it is on by the letters *CS* that appear on the status line.)

- You can use either the arrow keys or the mouse to extend the highlight over the column.

Not all columns are going to have smooth edges. In most cases, this won't make any difference, because you will be able to put the highlight over all of the column with little difficulty.

For sorting, calculating, or character formatting, all the text in a column entry must be inside the highlight. Anything not covered will not be included in the sorting, calculating, or formatting. The solution is to include the tab character that

133

Chapter 13

precedes the column text. To do this, you must have the command bar Options Visible display set to Complete.

For deleting or moving text, all of the text to be deleted or moved must be inside the highlight. The solution to this is to temporarily change the alignment to left justification. When finished inserting it elsewhere, restore the original justification.

Cutting a column from a table. Here are the steps for cutting a column of data out of a table:

- Set command bar Options Visible display to Complete.
- Put the cursor on the first character of the column to be deleted.
- Hold down the Shift key and press the F6 key. This turns on column selection.
- Use the arrow keys or the mouse to extend the highlight over the column. Be sure that it covers the trailing tab characters as well.
- If deleting the last column in a table, you must be careful not to delete the paragraph symbols or new line symbols. Deleting them will scramble the table. Use the space bar to line up all the paragraph marks or arrows, and keep the highlight to the left of them.
- Press the Del key.

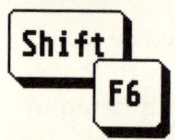

Any columns to the right of the one deleted will shift left to fill in the space vacated.

Paste a column. Before you paste a column into a table, you must make sure there is enough space for it to fit within the set margins and indentions. If not, make those adjustments.

- Delete the column with the steps listed in the previous subsection.
- Move the cursor to the first character or space that will be to the right of the inserted column. If pasting after the last column, this will be the new line mark symbolized by the down arrow. Use the space bar to line up all the arrows.
- Press the Insert key.

Pasting guidelines. If the table has been typed as a single paragraph, and you are pasting the column outside the table, you must use Shift-Enter to add new lines without a carriage

Making Tables of Information

return. This will insert the column as a single paragraph. Otherwise, each line of the column will use whatever paragraph marks that are available, and each line will be a paragraph.

The column space you are pasting into must have at least the same number of lines as what you are inserting. Otherwise, word-wrap may blend the text into other columns. If this happens, adjust the left and right indentions until the rows and columns match. You may even have to do some character deletion and retyping.

You must also be sure you are copying the column into the same type of tab alignment. For example, sending a left-justified column into a center- or right-justified tab zone can scramble the text. If you must attempt this, try changing the tab alignment. If that doesn't circumvent the problem, you may have to use the space bar and Tab key to straighten things out.

Copying a column to a glossary or text file. When you copy a column, you send a copy of it to the scrap. From there, you can either reinsert it elsewhere immediately or send it to more permanent storage in a glossary.

- Set command bar Options Visible display to Complete.
- Put the cursor on the first character of the column to be copied.
- Hold down the Shift key and press the F6 key. This turns on column selection.
- Use either arrow keys or the mouse to extend the highlight over the column. Be sure that it covers the trailing tab characters as well.
- Hold down the Alt key and press the F3 key. This places a copy of the marked text into the scrap.
- To put that copy into the document, move the cursor to the place you want to copy it, and press the Insert key.

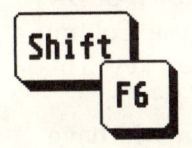

Chapter 13

- To copy it to a glossary, press the Esc key, type the letter C, give it a glossary name, and press the Enter key.
- To save it to a new text file, open a new window and clear it, copy the column into that window, and then save it as a text file.

To make the glossary permanent, you need to use the Transfer Glossary Save command.

You can also use this procedure for copying columns between documents in different windows. To learn how to use documents in different text windows, read the chapter titled "Using Multiple Text Windows."

Cutting and pasting or copying the rightmost column. There are special problems in cutting and pasting or copying the rightmost column in a table because the last column doesn't have trailing tab characters for you to mark and cut with the column. You also have to be careful not to cut out any down-arrow symbols representing new lines added with Shift-Enter.

You must insert trailing tab characters (down-arrow symbols) before you cut and paste or copy a final column. You can do this manually by putting the cursor after each entry in the column and pressing the Tab key.

You can do it automatically by aligning the down-arrow symbols into a column with the space bar. Then use Column Select to mark them as a column and press the Tab key. This will assign a trailing tab character to every down arrow.

If the column is center- or decimal-justified, it will have ragged lines. You can temporarily realign it as left-justified. Or you can use the space bar to align it and take out the extra spaces after it is moved.

Paste an existing column after rightmost column. You must understand the guidelines in the section above before reading this section.

The command bar Options Visible display must be set to Complete for these instructions to work.

- Check the margins and indentions to make sure there is room to add a column after the rightmost column. If there isn't, adjust them accordingly.

Making Tables of Information

- If this is a table typed as a single paragraph, use the space bar to align the down arrows that indicate a new line added with Shift-Enter.
- If this is a table typed with every line a paragraph, use the space bar to align the paragraph marks at the end of each line.
- Cut or copy the column from the table in the document.
- Put the cursor on the top of the column of new line arrows or paragraph marks.

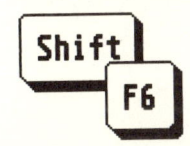

[Shift-F6]
- Use Shift-F6 to turn on the column-select mode and the down-arrow key to cover the line of marks.
- Press the Insert key.
- After the column is inserted correctly, go back and set a tab for that column.

Moving columns over to make room for a new column. Adding a new column to the middle of most tables is as simple as moving columns to the right to make room for the new one. Type the new column in the cleared space, and then adjust the tab settings as needed.

- Move the cursor to the upper left corner of the column to be moved right to make room for the new column.

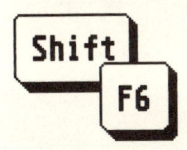

[Shift-F6]
- Use Shift-F6 to turn on column selection, and use the arrow keys or the mouse to cover that entire column.
- Press the Tab key. This should tab the columns to the right.

- Reset the tab stops to accommodate the new table layout.
- Type the new column in the empty space, but use the arrow keys to move the cursor from line to line.

Add a new column to the end of a table. The steps below can be used to add a new column to the rightmost side of an existing table. But they only work if there is room for the new column within the indents and margins. If there isn't room, then adjust them until there is enough room.

137

Chapter 13

To add a new column to the end of a table:

- Line up either the new line marks or paragraph marks at the end of each line.
- Add trailing tab marks to each line.
- Set a tab to accommodate the new column.
- Go back and and type in the entry for each line using the arrow keys to move to the tab positions in the new column.

Chapter 14
Using Borders and Lines

Borders and lines draw special attention to text on a printed page. If you put a box around a warning, note, comment, or heading, it will stand out from the normally printed text on the page.

Microsoft Word can provide borders or lines in the margin for your printed documents. It places a full selection of box- and line-drawing features at your fingertips.

Adding Borders with the Format Borders Menu

Microsoft Word offers a variety of options for drawing lines and borders in the text. The most important of these are offered through the Format Borders menu. The options on that menu allow you to do many things automatically. These features are actually a part of the paragraph formatting.

Different border types. *Microsoft Word* allows you to set automatic lines and boxes. These become part of the paragraph format and remain with the paragraph until you remove it. If you delete the paragraph, the box or lines go with it. If you move the paragraph, copy it, or save it to a file of its own, the paragraph will still have the assigned box or lines.

Different line style. *Microsoft Word* has three different line styles from which you may chose:

- Normal
- Bold
- Double

Normal. This prints lines in the single-strike or normal-printing mode for your printer. It will produce a line with the same darkness value as the regular text on your page. That will vary with the font, font size, and letter quality you're using.

Bold. This prints lines in the boldface mode of your printer. Most dot-matrix or daisywheel printers print boldface

139

Chapter 14

by restriking the letter once or twice on the paper. Some printers shift the printing slightly on succeeding passes, and thus make the line thicker. Laser printers do much the same in a single pass.

Double. This is double-line printing. Do not confuse it with double-strike printing. Double-line is done with high-bit ASCII graphics characters that print two lines side-by-side, a short distance apart. The border around the text window in *Microsoft Word* is done with double-line characters. So they will be displayed (even if they will not print as double—some printers are unable to produce double lines).

Printer and driver capabilities. If your dot-matrix printer has a NLQ (Near-Letter-Quality) mode, then some printer drivers will attempt to use NLQ to print these border lines, even if your text is printing in draft mode. This means it will be constantly switching back and forth between the two. This will slow down printing dramatically. The success it has with NLQ borders will depend entirely on the capabilities of the printer you're using. The better the printer, the better the results. Printers with 24-pin printheads give beautiful results. Laser printers will give you even better results.

Some printers cannot handle bold- and/or double-line printing at all. So you will get normal lines regardless of your settings. You should also be warned that different printers handle border printing in different ways. The line-drawing symbols are in the high-bit ASCII character set. Some printer drivers cannot process the high-bit characters. If it prints anything at all, it will print them as their low-bit text character value. Horizontal lines will print as *D*'s, vertical lines as 3's, and so on.

When any of these happen, it means:

- The printer driver you have installed cannot handle high-bit ASCII, even if it is the one meant for your printer. Try selecting a printer driver for a different model by the same manufacturer. If that doesn't work, try using the EPSONFX printer driver.
- If you have a 24-pin printer that you know is able to print true lines, then the printer driver is probably at fault. Try printer drivers for other printers by the same manufacturer. If

Using Borders and Lines

your printer is not one of the major brands, look for a printer driver for another manufacturer's printer with the same capabilities. Some drivers are better than others.
- Your printer cannot handle true-ASCII line drawing at all. Try setting up *Microsoft Word* to use the TTY driver. This will substitute text characters for the graphics ones. It won't be pretty, but it will do boxes and lines. If this doesn't solve the problem, all you can do is use another printer.

Setting paragraph boxes. These boxes are tagged to the paragraphs they enclose. They will expand as you type the paragraph or shrink as you delete it. You can cut and paste the paragraphs, and the boxes will go with them. If you change the margins, line spacing, indentions, any part of paragraph or division formatting, these boxes will adjust themselves to any changes you make. If you switch to multicolumn or side-by-side printing, the boxes will adapt to that as well. You can even use then for borders on an entire page of text by typing that page as a single paragraph.

- Put the cursor in the paragraph to be tagged with a border box.
  - Press the Esc key, and type the letters *FB*
  - Set type to Box.
  - Set line style to your choice.
  - Press the Enter key.

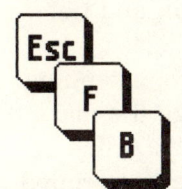

Paragraph border lines. These lines are also tagged to the paragraphs and are drawn automatically wherever you tell *Microsoft Word* to place them. They will expand as you type the paragraph or shrink as you delete it. You can cut and paste the paragraphs, and the lines will go with them. If you change the margins, line spacing, indentions, any part of paragraph or division formatting, these lines will adjust themselves to any changes you make. If you switch to multicolumn or side-by-side printing, the lines will adapt to that as well.

Chapter 14

This option has four variations:

Line on the left. This tags a paragraph with a line that prints down its entire left side. The most obvious purpose is to draw the eye to that paragraph, and thus give it special weight or consideration. Another good use for a vertical line is as a revision bar. Writers and editors use revision bars as a visual indication that the paragraphs have been rewritten or revised in some way.

Line on the right. This tags a paragraph with a line that prints down its entire right side. Use this in combination with a line on the left to make a paragraph really stand out from the page. It's also used by writers and editors as a revision bar, indicating changes to the paragraph.

Line above. This prints a line above the paragraph, extending from the left margin to the right. If you change the margins or indents, the line will adjust accordingly. A line above a paragraph separates it visually from the text printed above it. This is useful for marking the beginning of a section or subsection. It can also be used to mark off footnotes from the body text on the page. Just bear in mind that footnotes print in the bottom margin and not within the normal body text.

Line below. This prints a line below the paragraph, extending from the left margin to the right. If you change the margins or indents, the line will adjust accordingly. A line below a paragraph separates it visually from the text printed below it. This is useful for marking the end of a section or subsection. It can also be used for marking headings.

Setting up tagged lines. These automatic lines can be tagged to the paragraph either individually or in any combination you find useful or attractive. You can even use then for borders on an entire page of text by typing that page as a single paragraph.

• Put the cursor in the paragraph to be tagged with border lines.

Using Borders and Lines

- Press the Esc key and type the letters *FB*.
- Set type to *Lines*.
- Select the kind of line to be tagged by changing its answer to *Yes*.
- Set line style to your choice.
- Press the Enter key.

Removing paragraph borders. Any border box or line tagged to a paragraph can be removed by simply reversing the tagging routine. In this way, you can erase all or part of the border lines.

- Put the cursor in the paragraph with border box or lines to be removed.
- Press the Esc key, and type the letters *FB*.
- To remove all the borders, set type to *None*.
- To erase only selected lines, set them to *No*.
- Press the Enter key.

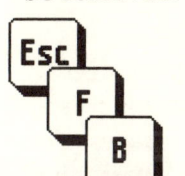

Removing all boxes and lines. If you want to remove all box or line tagging from a paragraph, there is a quick way to do it. It uses the fact that the box or line tagging is part of the paragraph format, and all paragraph formatting codes are tagged to the paragraph symbol.

- Put the cursor on the paragraph mark at the end of the boxed or lined paragraph.
- Press the Del key and then the Enter key.

This erases the paragraph formatting and replaces it with the paragraph formatting normal for the current page and division setup. If you have no special division formatting, the default settings will be used. This procedure is not recommended if you have given the paragraph any other special formatting, because that will erase as well.

If you change your mind before deleting anything else, you can always restore the deleted formatting by putting the cursor on the return mark at the end of the paragraph and

143

Chapter 14

pressing the Ins key. This can also be used to assign the identical border formatting to other paragraphs.

Cut and paste bordered paragraphs. The border boxes and lines are tagged directly to the paragraph. So you can cut and paste them exactly like any other paragraph text. But remember, the border tagging codes are assigned to the paragraph mark. If you don't cut and paste that paragraph mark too, the text will lose the box or lines.

- Use the mouse or the F9 and F10 keys to cover the paragraph to be cut.
- Press the Del key.
- Move the cursor to the place where the paragraph is to be pasted.
- Press the Ins key.

Connected boxes in boxes. There is a way to connect boxes around multiple paragraphs. The effect of this is to stack the boxes, one on top of the other, on the page or pages. This is useful for adding a boxed title to a boxed table, chart, illustration, or list. Or it can be used for separating information and categories vertically in the document.

- Type the paragraphs normally.
- Go back and delete the paragraph marks that separate them.
- You may want to type an unusual character, like an asterisk, as a visual reminder of where each of the paragraph breaks fell. You can delete this character prior to restoring the normal paragraph breaks.
- Tag this joined paragraph with whatever box type you want to use.
- Put the cursor on the first character of each original paragraph, and press the Enter key at each location.
- If your printer can execute double-line boxes, this will produce an especially pleasing effect. The box around all the boxed paragraphs will be double-line. But the lines separating the paragraphs will be single-line.

Boxes around multiple paragraphs. There is a way to fool *Microsoft Word* and put tagged boxes around multiple paragraphs or an entire page. This trick is not mentioned in the factory documentation.

- Type all of the paragraphs, or the entire page, as a single paragraph. You can tag each paragraph with a box either before or after you type it.
- Use new lines inserted with Shift-Enter for paragraph breaks.
- Insert paragraph indention with the default tab stops.
- You will have to turn on the line number display and watch for the bottom of the page. If there isn't room for the entire box on the current page, repagination will put a page break above the entire box and will send the whole thing to the next printed page.

Another way to do boxes around multiple paragraphs. You can also put a box around multiple paragraphs by following these steps:

- Remove the paragraph breaks between paragraphs already typed.
- Tag lines above, below, left, and right of the merged paragraph.
- Restore the paragraph breaks with carriage returns.

This gives you:

- A top paragraph with lines left, right, and top.
- A bottom paragraph with lines left, right, and bottom.
- Any paragraphs in the middle will have left and right lines.

Microsoft Word has been fooled into merging the lines continuously all the way around.

Boxes around empty space. You can put boxes around space left vacant so an illustration can be added later. This involves assigning a box tag to a solitary paragraph mark, then adding new lines to the empty paragraph with Shift-Enter.

- Place a paragraph mark at the beginning of the space where you want to insert the empty box.
- Put the cursor on that paragraph and tag it with the kind of box you want it to have.

- Hold down the Shift key and press the Enter key to add lines without a carriage return. Keep adding lines until the empty box is as tall as you want it.

Guidelines for empty boxes. Don't let the box cross a page break. Repagination will send all of the box to the next page. The box will use the currently set left and right margins as defaults. If you want it to be wider or smaller, change the paragraph indents. You can also use the indents to change the horizontal placement of the empty box. You can use negative numbers in the right paragraph indent to set it wider than the surrounding text.

Don't set the box to print wider than the paper you have *Microsoft Word* set to print on. The printer will break off everything that extends past the extreme printing limits. Anything broken off this way will be wrapped to succeeding lines.

Drawing Lines with Tabs

Microsoft Word's tab options have built-in line drawing capabilities. These are covered in depth in Chapter 12, "Setting and Using Tabs," so they will only be repeated in this section as brief overview.

Vertical lines with tab stops. You can set a vertical tab that will automatically draw a line vertically between columns or through the lines of text. These lines are drawn with the graphic character for vertical lines. Not all printers can process these high-bit ASCII characters. If your printer doesn't have graphics capability, then you cannot print them.

Horizontal lines with tab stops. You can set any tab to draw horizontal lines between tab stops. Those lines can be drawn with the period, the hyphen, or the underline character. When these are attached to a tab stop, they are called *leader characters*, because they lead you from point to point. Any printer can print these horizontal lines.

If you have your command bar Options Visible display set to Complete, your monitor may not display leader characters. Change the display to Partial; they should appear.

Using the Line-Drawing Mode

Microsoft Word has a line-drawing mode that can be toggled on and off with Ctrl-F5. This mode can be used to draw horizontal and vertical lines directly into the document. Those can be very useful tools in preparing special purpose documents

These lines are not tagged to any particular paragraph. They are inserted as ASCII graphics text into the body of the document. This means you can use the mode to draw the boxes onscreen, then go back and use the overtype mode to type text into the boxes. With this, you can produce graphics displays like organizational charts and flowcharts.

Unfortunately, their use is handicapped by several shortcomings. The drawing features are not put on their own graphics menu. Instead, you must select the drawing point or brush as a line-draw character through the command bar by calling the Options menu. From there, you call yet another list by pressing the F1 key.

Once you've selected the character, you can't use the mouse for drawing these lines. In fact, the mouse driver is completely cut off from access to the text window when the line-draw mode is toggled on. You can only draw using the cursor keys, so you are limited to strictly horizontal and vertical lines.

Unfortunately, *Microsoft Word* doesn't have a built-in graphics printing routine for printing graphics characters on a nongraphic printer. On many dot-matrix printers, *Microsoft Word* will print these high-bit ASCII characters as their low-bit characters (letters and numbers). So you'll wind up with letters and numbers where you intended to print lines and borders.

If, on the other hand, you have a graphics-capable 24-pin or laser printer, you can produce highly attractive boxes, lines, flowcharts, and interesting backgrounds.

Selecting the line-draw character. The line-draw mode has 12 different types of line-drawing styles from which you may choose. These are accessed and changed through the command bar Options menu.

Chapter 14

- Press the Esc key and type the letter O.
- Move the highlight to the selection labeled *linedraw char*.
- Press the F1 key to call the list of line-draw characters.
- Use the arrow keys or the mouse to move the highlight to the character of your choice.
- Press the Enter key.

Guidelines to the line-draw characters. The top three selections on the list represent sets of line-drawing characters. They have different characters for horizontal and vertical lines, corners all around, and lines drawn perpendicular to another line. With the others, the same character is drawn whether you move across or down.

The Hyphen/Bar set and the period are low-bit characters from the ASCII list, and they can print on any kind of printer. The others are high-bit ASCII graphics characters and require a graphics printer to print them. The average dot-matrix printer cannot handle them. To print these on a daisywheel printer, you must pause the printer and swap print wheels, then pause and swap when the graphic is done.

Drawing the lines. As mentioned above, the mouse can't be used to draw lines. You can still see and move the mouse pointer onscreen, but clicking the buttons will have no effect. These lines can only be drawn with the cursor movement keys. Generally, the point at which drawing takes place is refered to as the *penpoint*. In this case, the penpoint and the cursor are the same thing.

- Select the line-draw character set you want to use.
- Put the cursor at the place where you wish to start drawing.
- Hold down the Ctrl key and press the F5 key. This toggles on the line-draw utility.
- Use the cursor movement keys to draw the horizontal and vertical lines.
- When finished, or when ready to change drawing points, toggle the line-draw mode off with Ctrl-F5.

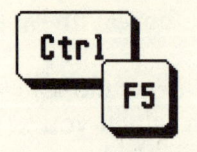

148

Table 14-1. Line-Draw Commands

Command	Effect
Ctrl-F5	Toggles the line-drawing mode on and off
Arrow keys	Draws line in direction of arrow
Home key	Draws a line from cursor position to paragraph's left indent.
End key	Draws a line from cursor position to paragraph's right indent.
Esc key	Exits line-drawing and activates command bar.

Moving without drawing. If you don't want to draw over other lines with the current one, you must lift the penpoint before you move to a different drawing location. To lift the penpoint you must exit from the line-draw mode. To do this:

- Toggle the line-draw mode off with Ctrl-F5.
- Use the cursor movement keys to put the cursor in the next place where you want to start drawing.
- Toggle the line-draw mode back on with Ctrl-F5.

Moving the penpoint with the mouse. The only way to use the mouse in drawing lines is to quickly move the penpoint to a new location. You must escape from the line-drawing mode before you can do this.

- Toggle the line-draw mode off with Ctrl-F5
- Move the cursor to the desired location.
- Click the Left Button to fix the cursor.
- Toggle the line-draw mode back on with Ctrl-F5.

Erasing lines. These lines are drawn with text characters, so you can erase them, copy them, and move them like normal text. If you make a mistake, use Ctrl-F5 to toggle out of the line-draw mode. Then use the standard delete, copy, and insert routines. You will notice as you delete that deleting line segments removes character spaces from the line. You can replace them with the space bar and realign the borders you have drawn.

Guidelines for text inside a border. The following notes will help you draw border lines.

- Don't try to draw lines around existing text. This will only cause problems.
- Draw the border lines first in some empty part of the text

Chapter 14

file, and then use the overwrite mode to type the text inside the boxes or borders.
- Use the arrow keys to move around inside the boxes and borders. Using the Enter key will distort or word-wrap the lines.
- Use only fixed-pitch fonts inside these boxes or borders. Proportional-space fonts will completely ruin your efforts.
- Keep default formatting. Don't use paragraph formatting or styling tools like centering, indentions, and so on.

Chapter 15
Printing with *Microsoft Word*

Microsoft Word has the capability of using most printers to their limits. It also allows you tremendous flexibility. You can:

- Print any document in any active text window.
- Print multiple copies of any document, including merge printed documents.
- Print text directly from the keyboard as you type it.
- Change printers easily before printing the documents.
- Print not only standard documents but also the glossaries you have created.
- Use queued printing to print one or more documents while writing and editing another.
- Print hidden text and summary sheets along with the normal text of the document.

Calling and Using the Print Menu

- Press the Esc key and type the letter *P*.
- To select any command option from the menu, either use the mouse or type the capitalized letter in the command.
- To escape from the Print menu, press the Esc key.

Normal Printing

The Print Printer command tells *Microsoft Word* to send the document in the active window to the printer. This is the most basic of the printing features. After you have written a document, or have loaded one into memory, execute this command to print a hardcopy of it.

Chapter 15

If you're using multiple windows, you must be sure to activate the window with the document you want to print. The Print Printer command will print the document in the currently active window.

If you start the print run-off when the printer is turned off or is offline, *Microsoft Word* will flash the message: *Printer is not ready.* Then the message will change to: *Enter Y to continue or Esc to cancel.* If you want to print the document, then prepare the printer and answer *Y.* Otherwise, cancel the run off by pressing the Esc key.

Start normal printing. These are the steps for executing the most basic *Microsoft Word* print run-off. It does not include any of the printing options or variations. It prints the document as-is.

- Type or load the document into the text window.
- Press the Esc key and type the letters *PP.*

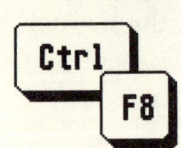

- You can also use the macro Ctrl-F8 to start the print run-off.

Pause or stop printing. You can pause and/or stop the print run-off with the Esc key.

- At any time while the printer is running, press the Esc key.
- *Microsoft Word* will display the message *Enter Y to continue or Esc to cancel.*
- If you do nothing further, a few more lines will print, and then the run-off will pause. Answer *Y* to start the printing again.
- If you press the Esc key a second time, the run-off will abort.

You don't have to wait for the message to appear. You can press the Esc key twice in quick succession. *Microsoft Word* will form feed to the end of the current sheet of paper. If you don't want that form feed, then turn the printer off and then back on.

152

Setting the Printing Options

The Print Options are the defaults *Microsoft Word* uses for printing the documents. When you change any of these options and then quit *Microsoft Word*, the new settings become the defaults. If you don't want an option change to become permanent, the restore it before you quit the program, or exit the program by reseting the computer.

Any or all of the printer options may be reset at one time while at the Print Options menu. You can have only one set of Print Options, no matter how many windows or printer ports you may have. Changing the print options while in any active window will change the options for all the windows.

Choose a different printer. While the highlight is on Printer, you can select another printer. To exit at any time without making changes, press the Esc key.

When *Microsoft Word* is set up to run on your computer, one printer is selected as the default. At the same time, others could be selected as alternates. It's fairly common to use different printers for different documents or tasks. To change the selected printer:

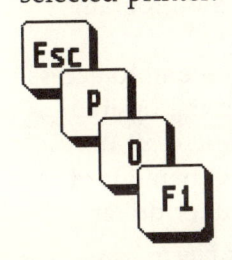

- Press the Esc key and type the letters *PO*.
- While the highlight is on Printer, press the F1 key. This will display the list of all the printer drivers that *Microsoft Word* has been set up to use.
- Use the arrow keys or the mouse to move the highlight to your selection.
- Press the Tab key or use the mouse to go to the next option.
- When ready to print, press the Enter key twice.

Guidelines for selecting printer drivers. If the printer you want to use is not on the list, look for a similar model by the same maker. All printers of the same type by the same maker share a common subset of printing and character set instructions. This will serve for most basic printing tasks. It won't necessarily provide all of your printer's special features.

If another printer by the same maker doesn't appear on the list, try using the EPSONFX.PRD driver. It is, in effect, an

Chapter 15

industry standard for basic printing. It may not access your printer's special features. It'll just run your printer as if it were an EpsonFX. Once again, this will serve for most basic printing tasks.

Many printers, especially laser printers, have special fonts on plug-in font cartridges. Each cartridge requires its own special printer driver before its fonts can be used. You must be very careful to use the right driver for the cartridge installed in the printer or the results can be disastrous.

Adding more printer drivers. When *Microsoft Word* is set up, only the printers selected at that time will be on the Print Options list of printers. If the printer driver you need is not listed, then *Microsoft Word* was not set up to use it. This doesn't mean you can't use it. It just means that the printer driver was not copied to your working disk from the master printer disks.

There are two different ways to add printer drivers to the list:

- You can add printer drivers to the list by going back through the setup utility. Exit *Microsoft Word* and run the program SETUP that is on the setup and utilities disk.
- The second method is to call the Library Run menu to access DOS; then use the Copy command to transfer the desired printer driver from the printers disk to your *Microsoft Word* disk or directory. If you don't know the correct name for the driver, use DIR/P to list a directory of the printer drivers.

Either method will get the job done. The SETUP routine is straightforward and dependable, but it means interrupting your work to use it. It's simpler to use DOS to copy in the printer driver you need.

Changing the printer port setup. When the highlight is on the setup option, you can select a different printer port. Press the F1 key and use the arrow keys to make your selection. The default printer port for *Microsoft Word* is COM1. You may have to change this if you are using a mouse.

Printing with Microsoft Word

- Press the Esc key and type the letters *PO*.
- Move the highlight to Setup.
- Press the F1 key to display the list of communication ports.
- Use the arrow keys to make your selection.
- Press the Tab key or use the mouse to go to the next option.
- When ready to print, press the Enter key twice. To exit at any time without making changes, press the Esc key.

Guidelines for selecting printer ports. The computer uses the printer control board to talk to the printer (and the rest of the outside world). Most printer control boards have at least two communications ports. These are commonly set up to be a parallel port and a serial port.

If yours has only one, then it will be the one made specifically for your printer. In order to have a selection, you must either get a bus mouse or install another parallel/serial board in your computer.

Microsoft Word can use the following ports: COM1, COM2, LPT1, LPT2, or LPT3.

If you're using a nonbus-type mouse, it's probably plugged into the COM1 port. Either reinstall the mouse or select the LPT1 port as the port your printer will use.

If this sounds confusing to you, read your computer's manual or talk to your dealer. Find someone with experience to help you.

Printing multiple copies. When the highlight is on the Copies option, you can tell *Microsoft Word* how many copies of the document you want printed. The default is one copy. You can print as many copies as you want. When multiple copies are printed, *Microsoft Word* prints all of the first copy, then all of the next, and so on.

When you finish printing multiple copies, return to the Print Options menu and restore the default to one. Otherwise, you'll print multiple copies of everything you print from then on.

Chapter 15

- Press the Esc key and type the letters *PO*.
- Move the highlight to Copies. The default should be 1.
- Type the number of copies you want to print.
- Press the Tab key or use the mouse to go to the next option.
- When ready to print, press the Enter key twice.
- To exit at any time without making changes, press the Esc key.

Selecting draft or full-feature printing. When the highlight is on the Draft option, you can toggle between the draft mode and the full-feature mode of your printer. The draft mode is the simplest printing your printer will execute. If you have a near-letter-quality printer, this is where you tell *Microsoft Word* whether to use.

- Press the Esc key and type the letters *PO*.
- Move the highlight to Draft. The default should be set to *No*.
- Answer *Yes* for Draft mode or *No* for full-featured printing.
- Press the Tab key or use the mouse to go to the next option.
- When ready to print, press the Enter key twice.
- To exit at any time without making changes, press the Esc key.

Printing hidden text. Hidden text is a Format Character option. It tags the text to become invisible to the printer during the run-off. But you can tell *Microsoft Word* to print the hidden text. Most of the time, you will not want to do this, so the default should be set to *No*.

- Press the Esc key and type the letters *PO*.
- Move the highlight to Hidden Text. The default should be set to *No*.
- Answer *Yes* to print hidden text; *No* if you don't want to print it.
- Press the Tab key or use the mouse to go to the next option.
- When ready to print, press the Enter key twice.

Printing with Microsoft Word

To exit at any time without making changes, press the Esc key.

Print summary sheet. When the highlight is on Summary Sheet, you can decide whether to print the document's summary sheet along with it. If you have not attached a summary sheet to the document, this option will have no effect.

- Press the Esc key and type the letters *PO*.
- Move the highlight to Summary Sheet. The default is usually set to *No*.
- Answer *Yes* to print the summary sheet; *No* if you don't want to print it.
- Press the Tab key or use the mouse to go to the next option.
- When ready to print, press the Enter key twice.

To exit at any time without making changes, press the Esc key. The summary sheet option is turned on or off at the main Options menu.

The printing range variations. When the highlight is on the range option, you can control the scope of *Microsoft Word's* printing with any document. This printing range allows you to print as much or as little of the document as you need or want.

All. This tells *Microsoft Word* to print the entire document from beginning to end.

Selection. This tells *Microsoft Word* to print only the selection of the document that you have covered with the cursor highlight.

Pages. This tells *Microsoft Word* to print only the pages of the document you have specified. You can print a selection of individual pages, groups of pages, combinations of groups and individual pages, a page or group of pages within specific divisions. No other program gives you such complete control over printing pages from a document.

Printing the whole document. The default printing sends the entire document to the printer at printing time. This will begin with page 1 and will continue to the end of the document.

Chapter 14

- Press the Esc key and type the letters *PO*.
- Move the highlight to Range.
- Answer *All* to print the entire document.
- Press the Tab key or use the mouse to go to the next option.
- When ready to print, press the Enter key twice.

To exit at any time without making changes, press the Esc key.

Printing selected text. This option will allow you to print only specific paragraphs and sections from a document. This is useful for producing excerpts from a document. You won't have to print an entire page to print a specific paragraph. You can also excerpt a specific section from the document and print it as a document in its own right.

- Use the function keys or the mouse to mark the selected text you want to print.

- Press the Esc key and type the letters *PO*.
- Move the highlight to Range.
- Set the option to Selection.
- Press the Tab key or use the mouse to go to the next option.
- When ready to print, press the Enter key twice.

To exit at any time without making changes, press the Esc key.

Printing selected pages. Before you can specify selected pages in a document, you must use the Print Repaginate command to set the page breaks in the document. Otherwise, you can't really be sure where the pages actually occur.

- Press the Esc key and type the letters *PO*.
- Move the highlight to Range.
- Set the option to Pages.
- Press the Tab key or use the mouse to go to Page Numbers.
- At Page Numbers, type in the specific pages or groups or pages from the document that you wish to print.
- When ready to print, press the Enter key twice.

Printing with Microsoft Word

To exit at any time without making changes, press the Esc key.

Guidelines for printing selected pages. Printing selected pages from a *Microsoft Word* document is a two-step process:

- At the Range option, tell *Microsoft Word* to print Pages.
- At Page Numbers, tell *Microsoft Word* which pages you want it to print.

With this option active, *Microsoft Word* will print only the pages of the document that you specify.

- You can print a string of individual pages (put a comma between each one, as in 1,3,5,7,9).
- You can print a group of pages (put a colon or hyphen between the first and last page numbers in the group you want to print, as in 5:9 or 5-9 to print pages 5 through 9).
- You can print combinations of groups and individual pages (by using the above syntaxes together as in 1,3,5-9,13,17,19).

If the document has multiple divisions, with different page numbering in each, you can print a page or group of pages within specific divisions: Type the page number first, followed by *D* or *d;* then type the division number, as in 1d3 or 5D2 or 9d1. You can also print a group of page and division numbers by using the above syntaxes together as in 9d1-5d2, 7d1:21d4. It doesn't make any difference whether you use a colon or a hyphen to separate beginning and end numbers. It doesn't make any difference whether you use capital or lowercase *D*'s to designate divisions.

Using widow and orphan control. An *orphan* is the first line of a paragraph appearing at the bottom of a page. A *widow* is the last line of a paragraph appearing at the top of a page.

- Press the Esc key and type the letters *PO*.
- Move the highlight to widow/orphan.
- Answer *Yes* to turn it on, *No* to turn it off.
- Press the Tab key or use the mouse to go to the next selection.
- When ready to print, press the Enter key twice.

159

Chapter 15

To exit at any time without making changes, press the Esc key.

Ways to control widows and orphans. There are three different ways to control widows and orphans:

- Manually, by watching where the page breaks fall when you repaginate the document. If you see an orphan, issue carriage returns to move the orphan below the page break. If you see a widow, insert a page break higher in the paragraph. If the paragraph is only a few lines long, put the page break above it. Repaginate as necessary.
- Use the Keep Follow command found on the Format Paragraph menu. With that command, if the first two lines of the second paragraph can't fit at the bottom of the page, then the last two lines of the first paragraph will be printed at the bottom of the next page.
- Automatic widow and orphan control works during the print run-off. If there isn't enough room on the page for the entire paragraph, the whole paragraph will be moved to the next page. If printing text in columns, the paragraph will move into the next column.

Guidelines for widow and orphan control. Automatic control will make awkward breaks that leave too much empty space at the bottom of a page. If the page count is important, or if you want to print a constant number of lines on each page, then you're better off controlling this manually or with the Keep Follow option.

Automatic control can break apart other text that you may want to keep together. This can be in the middle of a table, a list, or in the middle of a paragraph that will lose effectiveness if split between two pages.

Varying the paper feed. Different printers use different methods for feeding the paper past the print head. *Microsoft Word* has been written to use the most standard methods of the printers it supports.

Printing with **Microsoft Word**

- Press the Esc key and type the letters *PO*.
- Move the highlight to Feed.
- Select either Manual, Continuous, a specific Bin, or Mixed.
- Press the Tab key or use the mouse to go to the next selection.
- When ready to print, press the Enter key twice.

To exit at anytime before starting the printing of a document, press the Esc key.

The different types of feed. There are several different kinds of paper feed available. Here are the ones that can be used with *Microsoft Word:*

Manual. Load each sheet of paper by hand into the printer.
   Use this when printing letters or important documents on quality paper.
Continuous. This tells the computer it is using standard continuous, sprocket-fed computer paper.
Bin1. If the printer has a paper bin or tray designated as Bin1, this will tell *Microsoft Word* to use it during printing.
Bin2. If the printer has a paper bin or tray designated as Bin2, this will tell *Microsoft Word* to use it during printing.
Bin3. If the printer has a paper bin or tray designated as Bin3, this will tell *Microsoft Word* to use it during printing.
Mixed. This should tell *Microsoft Word* to feed paper from Bin1 until empty, then move to Bins 2 and 3 if they exist.

Guidelines for selecting paper feed. You need to know what kind of printer you are using before selecting the type of paper feed for *Microsoft Word* to use. If the printer cannot perform a specified type of feeds, the document may not print.

Most dot-matrix or daisywheel printers allow either manual or continuous feed as a standard feature. But some printers allow only one or the other. Only laser printers, and other expensive printers, have more than one paper bin.

Some companies require different kinds of documents to be printed on different kinds of paper. It's your responsibility to know what paper is in each bin and to match the document

161

Chapter 15

with the proper paper. If you're using a simple laser printer (like the Hewlett-Packard LaserJet models) with only one paper bin or tray, tell *Microsoft Word* to use standard continuous feed. These printers won't recognize bin commands.

Direct Printing from the Keyboard

You can print your document as it is entered from the keyboard almost as if you were typing it on a typewriter.

Print direct. Here are the steps necessary to print as if you were typing on a typewriter.

- Get the printer ready and online. Position the paper in the printer.
- Press the Esc key and type the letters *PD*.
- Carefully type the text.
- When finished typing, press the Esc key.

Guidelines for direct printing. The Print Direct command opens a clear line from the computer to the printer. Anything you type at the keyboard will be printed immediately. This is useful if you need to type something very short, like an address on an envelope.

At best, direct printing is a novelty. You may or may not have any use for it. When you print directly, you are giving up all the features of word processing, and you'll have all the same problems you might have with a typewriter. If you make a mistake, it'll go directly onto paper. And it is much more difficult to correct those mistakes while the paper is still in the printer.

This feature should be avoided if you're using a laser printer. With most laser printers, pressing the Enter key at the end of a line or paragraph will signal the printer to eject the page.

Printing a Document to Disk

You can print to disk almost as if you were printing on a piece of paper. Simply print to a print file.

To use Print File. Here are the steps necessary to print directly to disk:

- Type or load the document into the text window.

Printing with **Microsoft Word**

- Press the Esc key and type the letters *PF.*
- Type in the name of the file you want the printing sent to. Use a new filename. Give it the extension .DOC if you want it to display on the list of files called with the F1 key.
- Press the Enter key.
- *Microsoft Word* will print a replica of the document to the specified filename.
- To view the replica, use Transfer Load to copy it into a text window.

Guidelines for print to disk. The Print File command is essentially a previewing feature. It enables you to print an exact replica of the file as it will appear on paper, but the printing is done into another text file rather than on paper. *Microsoft Word* executes the print routine normally, but the file is sent to a disk drive instead of to the printer. This results in a text file that you can load into a window for viewing, writing, and editing.

This Print File feature is especially useful for test printing documents as you are learning to use *Microsoft Word.* Some of the more complicated formatting features are a bit tricky to learn to use. If you are doing precision layouts for camera-ready copy, it often boils down to trial and error. You can waste a large quantity of paper in a short time.

Microsoft Word will print to a file at electronic speed, with no wasted paper. You could also use it to print a single form letter or contract from a mailing list data file.

If you want the preview file printed on another disk drive, then type the drive name as a prefix to the filename you use.

Printing Glossaries

If you have glossaries written and saved to any style sheet, you can print them out as a record of the text they contain. This can be done with any set of glossaries attached to any document or style sheet.

Print glossary. Here are the steps necessary to print a glossary:

163

Chapter 15

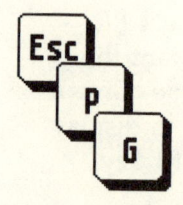

- Make active the window with the glossaries you want to print.
- Press the Esc key and type the letters *PG*.
- Type *Y* to continue or press the Esc key to cancel.
- All the glossaries will be sent to the printer.

Printing Form Documents

Merge printing is a complicated and specialized form of printing. This section will give only the briefest descriptions of its use. Merge printing is used for printing form documents like standard contracts or agreement forms.

A master document is written to hold the boiler-plate text used in every copy of the form document. The master document also contains commands that tell *Microsoft Word* where to find the text to be merged into the document. Code names for information like names and addresses are placed in the body of this document. The names refer to categories of information in the data file.

A data file or data document is written to hold the mailing list or information. The information in the mailing list is organized in lines and columns. If you type information in the wrong column, it will ruin the printed document.

During merge printing, *Microsoft Word* reads the commands in the master document and prints its boiler-plate text. When a code name is encountered, *Microsoft Word* will search the data file for the corresponding text and then print that text in the hardcopy. In this way, a letter for every name on the mailing list can be custom printed.

Queued Printing with *Microsoft Word*

Queuing means to line things up. With queued printing, you can print one document while working on another. This is frequently called *printing in the background*. Queued printing is especially useful if you're in a networked system that shares a common printer.

You can send more than one document to the printer at a time. *Microsoft Word* will print them in the order you send them. The only limitations are the size of the computer's RAM

Printing with Microsoft Word

and the amount of available disk space. When queued printing is used:

- The files must be loaded into windows and then queued one by one.
- *Microsoft Word* makes a temporary printing file on the current disk. After the file is printed, it's deleted from the disk.
- If there is not enough room for a temporary file on the logged disk, the following error message will display: *Document disk full.*

When running the program from a two-floppy-drive system, you can try swapping document disks in and out during the printing. But this can cause enormous problems if you try to write and edit while printing. If you make changes that create .TMP files on disk or you save the file during printing, it will split your document up among different disks.

If your system has only one floppy drive and no hard drive, don't use queued printing for any but the shortest documents. To make room on your target disk, save the file(s) before printing. This should remove all the .TMP files from that disk. If your disk is still too full to use, copy the file(s) to a new disk and then load and print from there.

Running queued printing. Here are the steps to follow when you want to print queued files:

- Press the Esc key and type the letters *PO*.
- Move the highlight to Queued.
- Answer *Yes* to turn queued printing on, *No* to turn it off.
- Press the Tab key or use the mouse to go to the next selection.
- When ready to print, press the Enter key and then the *Q* key.

To exit at anytime before starting the printing of a queued document, press the Esc key.

Running multiple-queued printing. To print multiple-queued documents:

- Load each document into a separate window.
- One-by-one, activate each window and send its document into the queue.

Chapter 15

- *Microsoft Word* will print them in the order you sent them.
- To exit at anytime before starting the printing of a queued document, press the Esc key.

Setting the Pages in a Document

Pagination is the determination of where page breaks fall during the printing of a document. This is one area of *Microsoft Word* where what you see may or may not be what you get.

If a document has not been printed or repaginated, it will not have onscreen page breaks that reflect where the pages will actually break during the print run-off. Page breaks are never final until the document is sent to the printer. At that time, *Microsoft Word* reads the document and tells the printer where to insert the page breaks.

Microsoft Word does not have automatic pagination or repagination as you write and edit a document. Apparently, the wide variety of possibilities created by multiple division formatting make it too complicated to keep up with the pages automatically.

Every time you delete or insert text into the document, it changes the pagination. How much it's altered depends entirely on the size of the insertion or deletion.

Whenever you make substantive changes to a document with cut-and-paste, you should repaginate before printing the document. This is the only way that you can visually check the page breaks onscreen before you print the document.

Print repaginate. Here are the instructions for using the Repaginate command:

- Press the Esc key and type the letters *PR*.
- Answer *Yes* to confirm each page break before it is made, *No* to let *Microsoft Word* repaginate all the way through the document.
- Press the Enter key.
- When repagination is complete, the word count will display on the status line.

Word counting. The words in your document are counted automatically whenever the document is printed or the Print Repaginate command is executed. The word count will be displayed on the status line.

166

Chapter 16
Using Headers and Footers

One of the major selections on the Format menu is called *Running-head*. Microsoft lumped headers and footers together under this term. A *header* is text printed in the top margin on every page; a *footer* is text printed in the bottom margin on every page.

Headers and footers are used as references to the information contained within the page or to the chapter title. They can also be called a flip reference, because you can use them to track down specific information or passages as you flip through a book.

Using Headers and Footers

You can format any line or paragraph as a header or footer. They must be the first text on the page where you want them to begin printing. This can be at the beginning of a document or at the beginning of a new division.

Inserting a header. Here are the steps for inserting a header:

- Put the cursor highlight over the text to be a header or footer. 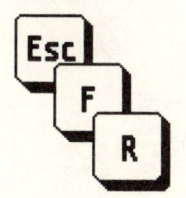
  - Press the Esc key and type the letters *FR*.
  - Set up the header or footer options. Choose top or bottom and what pages you want it to print on.
  - Press the Enter key.

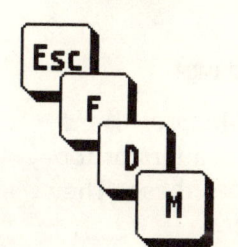

  - Press the Esc key and type the letters *FDM*.
  - Set the bottom margin to 1.25 inches and the running-head position from bottom to 1 inch. If this is too much, move it down.

Chapter 16

You can set up a header or footer to print only on odd pages, only on even pages, or on both. And it's common to omit headers from the first page of a chapter because the header usually echoes the chapter title.

The header or footer will appear on the designated pages to the end of the document or division or until it finds another header or footer setup for the same position and pages.

Displaying the header or footer status. *Microsoft Word* indicates that a header or footer is active by inserting a caret (^) at the leftmost side of the line on which the header or footer begins.

When you're working with headers or footers, you should turn on the style-bar display. This selection is found on the command bar Windows Options.

- Press the Esc key and type the letters *WO*.
- In the Style Bar option, answer *Yes*.
- Press the Enter key.

The widened space that opens down the left side of the screen is the style bar. It's used to display information about formatting that's inserted with style sheets and styles (Alt commands). In this case, *Microsoft Word* will display header or footer status by showing the style codes for the particular header or footer setup being used. Below is a chart of the codes and what they represent.

Style Code	Header/Footer	Page
tf	Header	First page
to	Header	Odd-numbered page
te	Header	Even-numbered page
t	Header	Odd- and even-numbered page
bf	Footer	First page
bo	Footer	Odd-numbered page
be	Footer	Even-numbered page
b	Footer	Odd- and even-numbered page

Speed-formatting headers and footers. *Microsoft Word* also has two commands for speed-formatting headers or footers. You may want to write down and remember these. They are Ctrl-F2 for a header and Alt-F2 for a footer.

Using Headers and Footers

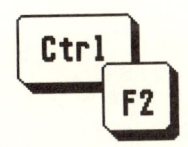

Ctrl F2
- For a footer, hold down the Alt key and then press the F2 key.

Alt F2
- Put the cursor highlight over the text to be a header or footer.
- For a header, hold down the Ctrl key and then press the F2 key.

Stacking headers and footers. If you're printing one-line headers or footers, you can stack as many of them as will fit in the margins. If the margins aren't wide enough, you can expand them. Each header or footer takes up only one line. You just have to remember to space each of them down from the top of the page so they don't overprint.

If you have any difficulty in placing them, try typing your measurements in lines (li) instead of the measurement standard you're using. *Microsoft Word* will automatically convert lines to the measurement standard you're currently using.

Making room for a header or footer. Whenever you are using headers and footers, you must remember to leave room for them to print. Headers are printed in the top margin of the page. Footers are printed in the bottom margin of the page. If you use more than one header or footer, you must adjust the margins to accommodate them.

The default header is set to print .5 inch down from the top of the page. The default footer is .5 inch up from the bottom. The default margins top and bottom are 1 inch. Sometimes this isn't enough room for even a single header or footer. If a simple header or footer won't print where you want it, widen the margin in .25-inch increments until it prints where you want it.

If you know how many lines your headers or footers require in addition to the default margin, type in the margins measurement in lines (li)—*Microsoft Word* will convert them.

Turning off a header or footer. If you decide you don't want a header or footer, you can either delete it like any other text or remove its formatting and return it to the body of the document.

169

Chapter 16

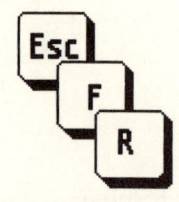

- Put the cursor highlight over the header or footer to be returned to normal text.
- Press the Esc key and type the letters *FR*.
- Select *No* for the options odd pages, even pages, and first page.
- Press the Enter key.

Headers and footers in divisions. *Microsoft Word* will not carry headers and footers over from the previous division. If you want to use the same running head in the following division, you must copy and insert it at the beginning of the new division.

Indenting headers and footers. The default setting for headers or footers allows them to use the entire width of the top or bottom margins. This means the right and left margins will be at the extreme limits your printer can print. The text will automatically realign to those margins in whatever justification status the paragraph already had. This will almost never be the way you want it to print. You must indent the headers and footers to print properly.

Headers and footers are formatted as paragraphs, so their indentions are set through the Format Paragraph menu.

- Press the Esc key and type the letters *FP*.
- Type in the measurements for the right and left indentions that will move the header/footer margins in from the edges of the page. The default margins for normal text are 1.25 inches.
- Press the Enter key.

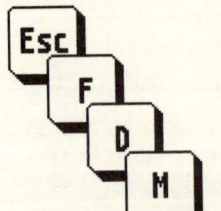

- Press the Esc key and type the letters *FDM*.
- Set the bottom margin to 1.25 inches and the running-head position from bottom to 1 inch. If this is too much, then move it down.
- Press the Enter key.

If you're printing standard single-line headers or footers, you must shift their right and left paragraph margins to print them where you need them. It will probably require some experimenting to get the exact look you want.

Using Headers and Footers

When printing even/odd headers or footers for back-to-back pages, you must either center-format the lines or set up a separate header/footer for left and right pages. When you do the latter, you must indent them to print where you need them. This may take some experimenting to get just the look you want.

If printing a banner head over multicolumn, or over side-by-side columns, then you should either center-justify it or indent it from the left the same distance as your body text. The default indent for regular body text is 1.25 inches.

If printing entire paragraphs as simple headers, or as banner text over multicolumns or side-by-side columns, you should give it the same left and right indentions as the body text of the document. The default indent for regular body text is 1.25 inches.

Positioning headers and footers vertically. If the default settings for header or footer position don't appeal to you, you can move them up and down in the margins by assigning each of them a different line on which to print. This is the same method used earlier to stack headers and footers in the margins.

The vertical position of the headers and footers is set up through the Format Division Margins menu. You may use any of the measurement scales that *Microsoft Word* recognizes.

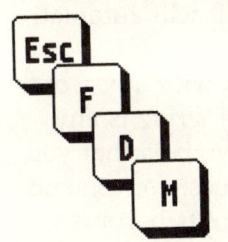

- Press the Esc key and type the letters *FDM*.
- Set the top and bottom margins to 1.25 inches, the header position to 0 inches from the top, and the footer position to 1 inch from the bottom. If this is too extreme, readjust the settings.
- Press the Enter key.

The default position for headers is .5 inch from the top. For footers, it's .5 inch from the bottom. Microsoft recommends that you set them no less than .167 inch (1/6 inch, or one line) above or below the regular body text.

Different headers and footers for odd and even pages. *Microsoft Word* allows you to set up different headers and footers for a document's odd- and even-numbered pages. This is often used to enhance the appearance of a book that's to be

Chapter 16

printed on back-to-back pages. Left pages commonly have the title and page number on the left side of the page. Right pages then have the title and page number on the right side of the page. When the pages are printed and bound back-to-back, the title and numbers fall on the outside edge. To accomplish this, you must set up two headers or footers to get the job done: one for left pages, one for right pages.

Formatting headers and footers as characters and text. What makes headers and footers special is that they can give your pages a special flair. Because headers and footers also format as paragraphs and characters, you can use those formatting commands to customize how the text itself will print. You can use different fonts and font sizes for headers and footers and give them character attributes that make them stand out from the page.

Headers and footers to identify the document. Headers and footers can also be used as a means of identifying your document. If you write documents for publication, you should know that many publishers require that you identify each page with a key word from the title, your last name, and the page number. If typing the manuscripts on a typewriter, you have to remember to include this information at the top of every page before you begin typing the body of page. With word processing, you can set up a header once and it will automatically print on every page.

You can identify each page of a document with any word, phrase, number, or character string (a *character string* is any group or series of letters, numerals, or other symbols that you can type on the keyboard). This reveals its greatest convenience in the event that pages from different manuscripts become mixed together. If you work with many different documents or send your manuscript to someone who does, this can happen easily. For your own convenience, you may want to put the chapter or section heads at the top of your long manuscripts. It can help keep you organized as you work on that document.

Page numbering with headers and footers. Page numbering with a header or footer gives you more flexibility than the standard page numbering. By numbering in a header or footer, you can put the numbers where you want them. You can also use different fonts and font sizes and different character and paragraph formats.

Microsoft Word uses merge-printing to print numbers in footers. You embed a code in the footer, and the current page number will substitute for it on every page.

- Format the header or footer.
- Put the cursor at the position in the header or footer where you want the page numbering to appear.
- Type the word *page*.
- Press the F3 key.

Microsoft Word will replace the word *page* with *(page)* in the header or footer. Then, during the print run-off, the page number for the current page being printed will be substituted in place of the symbol *(page)*.

If you want the word *page* to appear before the number, just type it in ahead of the symbol *(page)*.

Page numbering to identify chapters. You can use the above technique to give each chapter in a document its own special numbering format. This is used heavily in technical documentation. It's now common for user's manuals to have each chapter numbered in a characteristic style.

The state-of-the-art in high technology keeps changing rapidly. With each advance in the development of a machine or procedure, user's manuals have to be rewritten. The factory documentation for computer hardware and software often comes bound in loose-leaf notebooks. This allows the manufacturer to discard obsolete chapters or pages, replacing them in a short time. The alternative would be to reprint the entire book.

Chapter 16

- Set up your page numbering with the technique from the previous subsection.
- Put the cursor in the space before the symbol *(page)* and type the word, letter, or number that you want to use to identify the chapter. You can put a hyphen between it and the number.
- If this changes the formatting or indents, you must correct them.

You can use virtually anything you want to identify or customize the numbering of the chapters. It can be a key word from the title, the chapter number, or a code system of your own devising.

Chapter 17
Global Searches

All popular word processors have a feature with the generic name *global search*. A global search will look through a text file to find specific words or phrases. In other words, you can tell *Microsoft Word* to look for any word, phrase, sentence, or number in a text file, and it will search until it finds it.

Microsoft Word uses two commands for searching through text files for specific things. One is used to find words, phrases, or numbers. The other will help you find specific format attributes tagged to text.

Search features are extraordinarily useful. Once you understand how to use them and what they can do for you, they're certain to become an important part of your word processing repertoire.

Searching for Text

When looking for something in a printed document, you may very well have a general idea where the information you seek is located. You could flip through the pages quickly, trusting your eyes to pick out key words or phrases. In a nutshell, that's what the computer does for you with global search and replace.

For all practical purposes, the electronic document is invisible. The most you can see of it at any one time is a single text window on the monitor screen. When you want to find something in it, you have to scroll through it one text window at a time, going from page to page in the document, until you see what you're looking for.

Microsoft Word will do this for you. Just command it to find what you need, and it will do it.

Place markers in a text file. The most common use for the search command is to find a specific place in a text file.

Chapter 17

When you're working on a long document, it's sometimes difficult to keep track of the exact location of a piece of information, or where you left off on the previous day's editing or writing. If you know the page number in the electronic document, you can jump right to it. But when you cut and paste, revise, or add to a document, the page numbers themselves are likely to keep changing. The solution is to put place markers in your documents.

Section headings make excellent place markers. But don't limit yourself to that. You can use words or phrases as customized place markers in the document, and Search will go directly to them. Use your imagination. Make up a code of your own.

Marking places where you get stuck. When typing on a typewriter, you have to type every paragraph and section of it as a single document from beginning to end. That's the only way you can keep the paragraphs and sections in their correct linear progression. If a momentary lack of information or inspiration causes you to become stuck, you have to stop typing that chapter or section until you can become unstuck. As a result, useful writing time is squandered.

One of the benefits of a word processor is its ability to free your writing from linear restrictions. You don't have to write your whole document as a single continuous work. If you get stuck on a passage or you don't have the information you need, you don't have to stop writing. Leave a marker at the spot where additional work is needed and go on to the next passage. When you find a solution to the problem, search for the marker and fill in the gap.

Hidden text as a marker. You can use hidden text as a marker as easily as you can use printable text. In fact, hidden text is superior in many ways. It will keep the marker from printing if you make a hardcopy. Hidden text is a Format Character attribute. Just mark your place markers with the highlight and format them as hidden text.

The only catch to searching for hidden text is that the Window Options must be set to display the hidden text onscreen. If the hidden text display is off, then the Search command cannot find the hidden text.

You can search for:

- All occurrences of the same word or phrase.
- Specific sentences in a document. *Microsoft Word* can search for a phrase (or any other grouping of characters) as long as 253 characters.
- Formats and style tags. You can look for instances of boldfaced or underlined text.

The search options. Four of the five options that control the search can be found on the Search menu. The fifth is not.

Text. Text is the most fundamental option on the search process. This is where you tell *Microsoft Word* exactly what string of characters you're looking for. You can define the search to look for specific phrases or sentences.

Direction. You can set the search to go either down or up through the document. (If you are an old *WordStar* user, this is the same as going forward or backward, respectively.) The search will begin at the current cursor position and proceed to either end of the document. If you don't want to search through the entire document, move the cursor to the top or bottom of the portion to be searched, and then set the search direction accordingly.

Case. You can set the search to be specific or nonspecific to the case of the characters. You can find instances of capitalized words by specifying case, so you would find Desk-Top, for instance, and skip desktop, Desktop, dESKtOP and all other combinations of upper- and lowercase letters. Or you can tell *Microsoft Word* to ignore the capitalization status and just find the words. The latter is useful if you cannot remember how you capitalized the text in question. If you are searching for a word normally in lowercase, you will also want to use the nonspecific search because the word might appear at the beginning of a sentence and therefore be capitalized.

Whole word or part. You can make the search specific either to whole words or to parts of words. In most single-word searches, you should keep this set to whole words. There are many small words whose characters are contained

Chapter 17

within larger words. This consideration becomes crucial when doing search and replace through a document. For instance, if you're not using the Whole Word option and you replace *we* with *you*, you will end up with words like *howyouver* and *northyoust* in your document.
Specific selections. You can highlight the section to search within a text file, and the search will contain itself to that selection.

Using the search command. Use the command bar Search command to look for specific text. Your search is only restricted by what you type at the keyboard. If the text is in the document and it isn't double-hidden, *Microsoft Word* will find it.

To search through an entire document, put the cursor at either its beginning or end. The search will proceed from the cursor position in either direction through the file. If you put the cursor in the middle of the document, it will not search from beginning to end. This means you can designate major portions for search by your placement of the cursor. To search only a specific portion of a file, cover it with the cursor highlight.

- Position the cursor or cover the selection to be searched.
  - Press the Esc key and type the letter *S*.
  - Type the text for which you're searching. It must be spelled exactly as it exists in the document.
  - Select the direction—up or down—in which the search is to go. The default is set to *Down*.
- Set the Case option. *Yes* will tell it to search only for the text that exactly matches the capitalization of the search text. *No* will tell it to ignore case.
- Set the Whole Word option. *Yes* will tell it to search for the word only as a whole word. *No* will find the word, even if part of another word.
- Press the Enter key.

Searching for Formats

Microsoft Word allows you to give your text virtually unlimited combinations of character and paragraph formatting. With the standard monitor display, you can't see all the formatting tags. With an CGA or EGA display, the color coding gives you a clearer idea. But you cannot always tell by that. The more variations you use in a given document, the more confused you can become about where you have tagged them.

Format searching lets you to look for specific combinations of paragraph, character, or style tags. In this way, you can go directly to the text that needs additions or revisions.

Guidelines for format searches include:

- You can use the Format sEarch command to look for character or paragraph format tags that you designate.
- You can look for any text with the format tags for which you're looking, and *Microsoft Word* will ignore any unspecified formats.
- You can look for more than one character or paragraph format tag in any given search.
- Each major category of format search is executed through its own menu. You can only look for format combinations within a major category of character, paragraph, or style. You cannot look for combinations of character, paragraph, and style format tags.
- The style tags to be searched for are identified through their assigned keycodes. So you can only use the Format sEarch Style command to look for style tags that have assigned keycodes in the currently attached style sheet. The keycodes are defined differently from style sheet to style sheet. Some exist in one style sheet and not in another. If possible, try merging the style sheets.
- You can send the search in either direction through the document. The search begins at the cursor position and goes in the direction you specify. If you want to search through the entire document, put the cursor at the top or bottom of the file. If you don't want to search through the entire document, place the cursor where you want to begin the search, and

Chapter 17

send it in the direction you prefer. It will then search only the remainder or preceding portion of the file.
- You can restrict searches to specific portions of a text file by marking that selection with the cursor highlight. Then the search will be kept to that marked text.

Search for character format tags. Following are the steps you can use for initiating a search for specific character format-tags. Remember that this search looks for groups of tags. You must indicate the exact combination of format tags you're looking for.

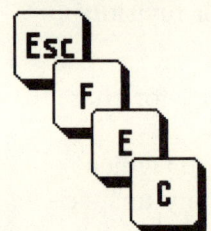

- Position the cursor or mark the selected text.
- Press the Esc key and type the letters *FEC*.
- Set the direction of search to Up or Down.
- Select the format tags for which you are looking.
- Press the Enter key.

Microsoft Word will search through the document, or the selected portion, until it finds the first group of characters with this tag combination.

Search for paragraph format tags. Below are the steps you can use for initiating a search for specific paragraph format tags. Remember that this search looks for groups of tags. You must indicate the exact combination of format tags for which you're looking.

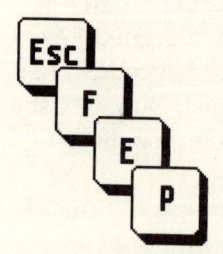

- Position the cursor or mark the selected text.
- Press the Esc key and type the letters *FEP*.
- Set the direction of search to Up or Down.
- Select the format tags for which you want to search.
- Press the Enter key.

Microsoft Word will search through the document, or the selected portion, until it finds the first paragraph with this tag combination.

Search for style tags. Below are the steps you can use for initiating a search for specific Style Tags. Remember that this search looks for groups of tags. You must indicate the exact combination of format tags for which you're looking.

- Position the cursor or mark the selected text.
- Press the Esc key and type the letters *FES*.
- Select the format tags for which you want to search. Do this by typing their keycode sequence.
- Set the direction of search to Up or Down.
- Press the Enter key.

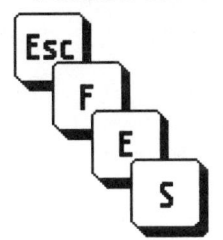

Microsoft Word will search through the document, or the selected portion, until it finds the first text with this tag combination.

Chapter 18
Global Search and Replace

A global search-and-replace will look for text in a document and replace it with different text. In other words, you can tell *Microsoft Word* to look for any set of characters and then specify the set of characters you want substituted for the original. *Microsoft Word* will search through the document for existing text and replace it with the text you have specified.

The search-and-replace feature is an extremely useful tool for writing and editing. These electronic searches have the ability to search the entire document for specific sets of characters. It can do this because every word, phrase, or string of letters and numbers has a unique ASCII coding structure. If you tell *Microsoft Word* to look for something, it looks for that unique sequence. If you tell it to replace that sequence with another, it will delete the old and type in the new. It can accomplish this literally in seconds.

Searching and Replacing Text

Here are the search-and-replace options available to you on the Replace menu:

Text. The first text field is for that text for which the search routine looks. Be sure to type the text exactly as it exists in the document. *Microsoft Word* will look for it exactly as you type it.

Text. The second text field is for entry of text to substitute for the text in the first field. Be careful to type it exactly as you want it.

Confirm: (Yes) No. If you answer *Yes, Microsoft Word* will ask you to confirm each replace before it's made. That way, you can replace some occurrences of text and leave some text the way it is. If you answer *No*, the search and replace will proceed throughout the document without stopping for confirmation.

Chapter 18

Case (Yes) No. You can set the search to be specific or nonspecific to the case of the characters. You can find every instance of a word or phrase regardless of whether it's capitalized, or you can tell *Microsoft Word* only to find those words that match the search string exactly. If you are writing an article about a man who drove his pickup across a shallow river, you might say *he forded the stream with his Ford*. If, later, you discover that he was driving a Chevrolet, you wouldn't want the search-and-replace feature to change the sentence to *he Chevroleted the stream with his Chevrolet*. Making the search-and-replace case-specific avoids this sort of mistake.

Whole word (Yes) No. This makes the search specific to either whole words or parts of words. In single-word searches, keep this selection to *Yes*. There are many large words that contain small words. This would also avoid the error mentioned above because *ford* is only part of *forded*.

Specific selections. Another option not on the search-and-replace menu is the simple fact that you can mark specific selections to search and replace within a text file. These selections are made in the normal way, by covering the passage with the cursor highlight. Search and replace will restrict itself to that selection.

Using the Replace command. The Replace command will find specific text and replace it with other text. Your only restrictions are what you type at the keyboard and whether it's double-hidden. If it's in the document and is not double-hidden, *Microsoft Word* will find the text and replace it with what you want in its place.

You can designate major portions for search by your placement of the cursor. To search only a specific portion of a file, cover it with the cursor highlight.

- Position the cursor or highlight the selection to be searched.
- Press the Esc key, and type the letter *R*.
- At the option Text, type the text for which you're searching. It must be spelled exactly as it appears in the document.

Global Search and Replace

- At the option With Text, type the new text to be inserted in place of the old.
- Set the Confirm option. The default will always be *Yes*. If you want the change to be made without your input, you'll have to change this option each time you search and replace.
- Set the Case option. *Yes* will tell it to search only for the text that exactly matches the capitalization of the search text. *No* will tell it to ignore case.
- Set the Whole Word option. *Yes* will tell it to search for the word only as a whole word. *No* will find the word, even if it's part of another word.
- Press the Enter key.

If you don't want hidden text included in your search and replace, then double-hide it by turning off the hidden text display on the Window Options menu.

Searching and Replacing Formats

With *Microsoft Word*, you can give Characters, Paragraphs, and Divisions virtually unlimited combinations of format tags. This is usually done as you type the document word by word, paragraph by paragraph, and division by division. Even if you use style tags and style sheets, formatting takes place as you type the text.

No matter how well your monitor reflects what will be printed, there are three basic facts you must accept:

- You won't really know how something will look until you print it.
- You won't really know how you are going to like it until you hold it in your hand.
- You will probably want to change some formatting elements throughout the document.

You'd probably ignore all but the grossest formatting errors if you had to correct them word by word, paragraph by paragraph, and division by division to make the format corrections. Fortunately, you don't have to: Format Replace is an editing tool that will do it for you.

185

Chapter 18

Guidelines for Format Replace. Here are the rules involved in searching for and replacing formats:

- You can replace any designated character or paragraph format tags, and *Microsoft Word* will ignore any unspecified formats.
- You can search for character, style, or paragraph tags and replace them with other character, style, or paragraph tags. But you can't mix these categories of tags. Each is executed through its own submenu.
- The Format Replace Style command only works for style tags that have assigned keycodes in the currently attached style sheet. The style tags are identified on this menu by typing in their assigned keycodes. Keycodes are defined differently from style sheet to style sheet. Some exist in one style sheet and not in another.
- A search and replace proceeds only in a downward (beginning to end) direction. The search begins at the cursor position and goes in the direction you command it. If you want to search through the entire document, put the cursor at the top of the file. If you don't want to search through the entire document, place the cursor where you want to begin the search.
- You can restrict searches to specific portions of a text file by marking that selection with the cursor highlight. The search will be limited to the marked text.

Search-and-replace character tags. The following steps execute a search and replace for specific character format tags. Remember that this search looks for groups of tags. You must indicate the exact combination of format tags for which you're looking.

This routine calls two different menus: a Format Search menu and a Format Replace menu. Take care to set each of them exactly as you want the routine to execute.

- Position the cursor or mark the selected text.
- Press the Esc key and type the letters *FLC*. This calls the menu for setting the character tags for which you want it to search.

Global Search and Replace

- Set the confirm to *Yes* or *No*.
- Select the format tags for which you want to search. Be very sure that you set it correctly.
- Press the Enter key. This calls the menu where you set the Character tags to replace the old ones.
- Select the Character tags to replace the existing ones. Again, make sure every tag is as you want it to be.
- Press the Enter key.

Microsoft Word will search through the document, or a selected portion, and will replace the character format tags as directed.

Search for paragraph format tags. These are the steps for executing a search and replace for specific paragraph format tags. Remember that this search looks for groups of tags. You must indicate the exact combination of format tags for which you are looking.

This routine calls two different menus: a Format Search menu and a Format Replace menu. Take care to set each of them correctly.

- Position the cursor or mark the selected text.
- Press the Esc key and type the letters *FLP*. This calls the menu for setting the character tags for which you want it to search.
- Set the confirm to *Yes* or *No*.
- Select the format tags for which you want to search. Be sure you set them correctly.
- Press the Enter key.
- Select the paragraph tags to replace the existing ones. Again, make sure you enter these correctly.
- Press the Enter key.

Microsoft Word will search through the document, or selected portion, and replace the paragraph format tags as directed.

Search-and-replace style tags. The following steps execute a search and replace for specific style tags. Remember that this search looks for groups of tags. You must indicate the exact combination of format tags for which you are looking.

187

Chapter 18

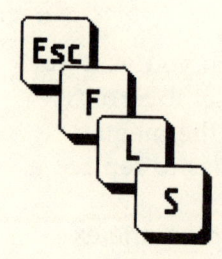

- Position the cursor or mark the selected text.
- Press the Esc key and type the letters *FLS*.
- Select the format tags for which you want to search. Do this by typing their keycode sequence, one by one.
- Press the Enter key.

Microsoft Word will then search and replace as directed.

Chapter 19
Using Multiple Text Windows

This chapter explains how to use *Microsoft Word*'s window capabilities. It's easy to use windows if you know what you're doing. If you don't understand single window operations, you have no practical use for this chapter.

A *text window* is the area onscreen where the text is typed and viewed. In its default setup, *Microsoft Word* displays the primary text window as a box bordered with a double line.

The term *window* is an apt one for describing the limitations of viewing a document onscreen. Even with the best monitors, most of the text file will always be invisible to you. With a word processor, you can only open a window on a piece of the text file, and then move the text through it a small amount at a time.

Opening More Than One Window

Microsoft Word boots up with only one window open. But you can open as many as eight windows and can load a separate document into each. This gives you the same effect as having up to eight word processors running at the same time. You can then write and edit up to eight documents at once, or exchange text among them as simply as working with a single text file.

When you have documents in different windows, you can cut and paste between one or all of them. When writing a new document, if existing documents contain text that can be used in a new one, you can copy any kind of text from an old document into the new. Just use the standard cut-and-paste routines.

Zooming in on the windows. The latest version of *Microsoft Word* (4.0) now has the ability to zoom in on each window you open. The ability to expand (zoom) an individual

189

Chapter 19

window is important because as you open more windows, the screen area available to each grows smaller. Editing and writing in a tiny window can be very uncomfortable.

When you zoom in on a window, the text in it will fill your entire screen. The window is displayed full-size. You can view it just as if it were the only file in memory. When finished, you can move to another expanded window or return all the windows to their reduced size.

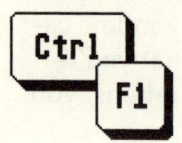

All it takes to zoom in or out of a text window is to hold down the Ctrl key and then press the F1 key. Then you can use the F1 key by itself to move consecutively through each of the windows you have open, zooming in on each of them in turn.

This makes it much more convenient to search through the text files for the passages you wish to find. It's easier to mark the text and to cut and paste it into the other text file where you need it.

A special reference-note window. When you use *Microsoft Word's* footnote/endnote feature, these reference notes are automatically inserted at the end of the document file. You may then select whether they are to be printed as footnotes or endnotes.

While writing and editing the footnotes/endnotes, you may find it inconvenient to jump to the end of the document every time. There is a special window you can open when working with reference notes. When you use this footnote/endnote window, the reference notes are kept onscreen all the time, displayed across the bottom of the screen.

This special window is particularly useful for keeping track of your notes. When there are very many in a document, this could be very difficult without the footnote/endnote window.

Display Modes

Microsoft Word has two distinct display modes from which you may choose. They are the Graphics mode and the Text mode.

These may be toggled through the main menu Options.

Just set display to either Graphics or Text. You may also select either as a part of booting up the program. At the DOS prompt (C: \ or A:), just enter the following:

- To start the program in Graphics mode, type *word/g*
- To start the program in Text mode, type *word/c*

When you quit *Microsoft Word*, whichever display mode it is in will become the new default setting.

The graphics display mode. The graphics mode is the standard display mode for the program. Your computer must have a graphics adapter installed to use it. This means that your computer must have either a color monitor or a dual-mode monochrome monitor. *Microsoft Word* will use the full graphics display capabilities of your monitor and graphics card.

In the graphics mode, *Microsoft Word* displays letters and numbers onscreen similar to the way they will appear when printed. Boldface will be intensified. Italic is slanted. Underlined and double-underlined text is shown with underlining. Strikethrough text is marked out onscreen. All of this makes it easier to visualize the printed version.

The text display mode. Text display gives the high-resolution display most monochrome monitors deliver. It's also a stripped-down display that allows *Microsoft Word* to work faster. In fact, that's its major advantage. The speed is gained because the computer no longer has to process all the complicated graphics codes used to provide a WYSIWYG display. This speedup is most noticeable in any routines that require redrawing the screen (scrolling through the document, for instance). It should also conspicuously speed up all global search-and-replace functions.

In the text mode, the graphics attributes of characters are not shown. With a color monitor, unformatted characters are only displayed in the normal foreground color. Various formats cause the text to appear in different colors.

On a monochrome monitor, boldface will be brightened and all character tagging (except font changes) will be underlined.

Chapter 19

If you have a mouse installed, the mouse pointer will be a blinking box instead of the familiar arrow. It will change height as it moves from place to place onscreen.

How to Use Multiple Windows

Believe it or not, working with multiple documents is only a little more complicated than working with a single document. Every window works exactly the same. Once you are familiar with the basic use of *Microsoft Word*, it's an easy step to go on to working with two, three, or more documents at the same time.

Actually, you aren't working with two or more documents at the same time. While the computer may display many windows containing documents, only one window is active for writing and editing at any time. So you're only working with one window or document at a time.

The routine for opening multiple windows. Here are the steps to follow in order to open (or *split*) multiple windows:

- Open the windows one at a time and load the documents into them one at a time. If you want to change the display settings for the windows, do so as you open them.
- Activate each window as you need to work in it.
- Cut and paste and revise according to your wish. Be sure to save all changes to each window document individually.
- Close the windows in the same order that they were opened. This will help you keep your default settings as you want them.
- When finished working for the day, use the Quit command to exit from *Microsoft Word*. Don't just turn off the computer, or you'll leave a lot of undeleted .TMP files on your disk.

Cut and paste between windows. Cutting and pasting between windows is one of the most powerful features of *Microsoft Word*. Here's how to accomplish it:

- Activate the window with the text to be cut.
- Select the text and send it to the scrap.
- Activate the window where the text is to be pasted.

- Put the cursor at the place where the text is to go.
- Press the Insert key.

Making a window active. A window is active when the cursor is in it. It's ready for writing and editing. You can also tell a window is active because its number will be highlighted. If you have the zoom feature turned on, making the window active will cause it to display full-size.

[F1] • Press the F1 key to cycle through the windows consecutively.

- If you have a mouse, just move the mouse pointer into the window and click the left button. If zooming is turned on, you'll have to move the pointer to the window number before clicking the button.

Two or more windows on the same document. If you don't clear a window as you open it, it'll be another window on the same document. While this may not seem important, it can be an extremely useful writing tool.

With a second or third window open on the same document, you can scroll to a different part of the document in each window without disturbing the display in the others. This allows you to look at different parts of the document at the same time.

Writing or revising a document usually means jumping back and forth inside the document. When you cut and paste to rearrange and reorganize a document, the procedure is to cut it, move the cursor, then paste it. You can do this the hard way, scrolling back and forth through the document, or you can open a window on each part, then cut and paste directly from window to window.

Another use for multiple windows on the same text is to compare different parts of a document side by side. During the writing of a long document, you may, without meaning to, be inconsistent with formatting and layout. By splitting a vertical window, you can display paragraphs or tables and compare them side by side for content or style. This is the next best thing to having a hardcopy and opening it to two different pages for comparison.

Chapter 19

Writing new drafts without changing the old. One of the housekeeping problems of working with a word processor is the need to keep separate drafts of your documents on disk. If you edit the version on disk, the original draft will be overwritten and replaced by the new.

For some users, this is not a problem. In fact, most writers probably blithely overwrite their previous drafts every time, particularly when they are doing informal writing, such as personal letters. But some work environments require a careful maintenance of each distinct draft. This is true in writing documentation for most government agencies, and for most large businesses, especially the ones doing contract work for the government. The purpose is to maintain a paper and electronic trail of all changes made. The government loves to keep track of accountability.

One solution is to open a new file, save it under a new name, then merge the previous draft into it. Then you can write and edit, and the previous draft will remain unchanged. When you do this, you must remember to keep a written log of filenames and their draft numbers. You should also attach a summary sheet to each draft, to match each draft with its entry in the written log. Finally, you should keep backup disks dedicated specifically to first draft, second draft, and so on. This ensures that nothing happens to the different versions of the document.

A variation on this practice is to open an empty window, save it under a different name, then merge the previous draft into it. Use all the other safeguards described above. The benefit is that you can display the old version beside the new and compare the revisions with the unedited text to see if you really want to rewrite it that way.

Cut-and-paste assembly. The kind of writing best suited to cut-and-paste assembly is standardized form documents. If you are a legal secretary, or a small business owner, you'll find yourself writing the same types of documents over and over again. Legal documents are so standardized that they seldom vary more than a few words or sentences in a hundred different printings. Most contracts, agreements, and release forms are as deliberately identical each time as is possible, simply to eliminate possible causes for disagreement or litigation.

If you are printing a large number of the same form documents, you should definitely use merge printing. But for printing only a few copies a day of several different kinds of documents, the cut-and-paste assembly method is unparalleled.

Boiler-plate and archive text. Reusable text is commonly called either *boiler-plate* or *archive* text. If you're just beginning with word processing, you probably won't have much of an archive of reusable text. But everything you type and save goes into the archive. If you have specific paragraphs, tables, or lists that are reusable, you can either save them to separate files or use multiple windows to transfer them into your new documents.

If you're working in an office environment or a documentation department, others before you have probably written a storehouse of boiler-plate text. With multiple windows giving rapid and simple access to many files at once, it's possible to assemble entire documents with cut and paste and little original typing.

Opening New Windows

Microsoft Word boots up with a single text window open. But you can open as many as seven more, for a total of eight. And you may, with limitations, open a separate text file in each window. The primary limitation is always the amount of memory in your computer. *Microsoft Word* uses a lot of RAM just to run. Each text file takes up more. So the secondary limitations are the sizes of the files you load into the windows. The bigger the files, the fewer you can work on at once.

You can correct much of this problem by expanding your computer's memory to 640K. Most AT-style computers can be easily expanded to more than a megabyte of memory. And there are low-cost memory expansion boards available for all PC computers. With these, you can add one or two megabytes of memory by simply plugging the boards into an empty slot on your main board and then setting up the system to use the memory.

195

Chapter 19

Avoid large text files in secondary windows. The simplest, and least expensive, way to avoid memory deficiency is to avoid working with large files in your secondary windows. The bigger a file, the more difficult it is to work with. It takes longer to load it, longer to save it, and longer to move around in it. In a large file, you can easily lose track of where you are and where to find the text for which you're looking.

As you build your archive of reusable text, set yourself up for the long term. If you have text you'll use again and again, divide it into smaller files that are easier to work with.

Avoid using text files larger than 50K in secondary windows. That is a good, convenient-size file to handle. In most cases, it works out to be the maximum with which you can work before encountering irritating time lags when working with the secondary files.

Splitting a window with the mouse. The simplest way to open another text window is with a mouse. All you do is point and click. This will open both vertical and horizontal windows. The window borders must be turned on for you to be able to split a window with the mouse.

- Move the mouse pointer to the top or right edge of any window where you want to split another. The arrow will turn into a small box.
- Position the box at the exact point where you want the window to split.
- Click the left mouse button.
- The window will split at that point.

Guidelines for splitting windows. Here are the rules that govern splitting windows:

- The pattern you make while splitting windows has an influence on how many subsequent windows you can open and where they may be opened. Sometimes you won't be able to open eight.
- You can only open three windows side by side. Each must be large enough to display the borders, the selection bar, the style bar, and at least one character. This generally means no closer than one-half to three-quarters of an inch apart. Each

horizontal window must take up a minimum of three lines onscreen.
- You cannot split a window to the left of the left margin.
- If you try to split a window where *Microsoft Word* can't open one, it'll display the message *Not a valid window split.*
- If you're planning to work with several documents at once, load each window before opening the next. This will let you know immediately when you're exceeding the memory limits.
- If using the outline mode while writing a document, open two windows on that document. Then keep the document in the second window permanently collapsed to its outline view as you write. The outline view will let you keep an eye on the structure of the document and will let you know when organizational changes need to be made.
- Keep a window open for making notes as you write and edit your document.
- When working with form letters, keep the master document in the primary window and the data file in a secondary. You can print with both in memory, instead of having the Print Merge routine search a disk. Be sure that the master document window is the one active when you execute the Print Merge command.
- You can open two windows on the same document, then display hidden text in one and double-hide it in another. This lets you see your hidden comments in one window and preview the printed version in the other.
- If you have only one window onscreen, you can turn off its borders with the Options menu. When you open a secondary window, the borders will reappear. But when you close the last secondary window, the primary window will return to its unbordered state.
- Unless you clear a window as you open it, it'll always be open on the document in the window in which it is split.

Splitting a vertical window from the keyboard. It's slightly more cumbersome to split a window from the keyboard. You must set each window individually with the same routine. But you have the benefit of putting each of them exactly where you want it.

Chapter 19

- If you already have more than one window open, use the F1 key to activate the window in which you plan to open the vertical window.

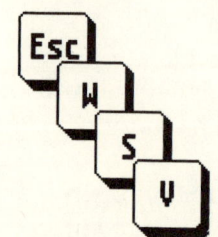

- Press the Esc key and type the letters *WSV*.
- In the At Column selection, type the column number in the active window where you want the new window to split.
- If you want to clear the new window as you split it, answer *Yes* at clear new window.
- Press the Enter key.

Splitting a horizontal window from the keyboard. Here's how to split a horizontal window (a window whose new restriction is a top border) from the keyboard:

- If you already have more than one window open, use the F1 key to activate the window in which you plan to open the horizontal window.

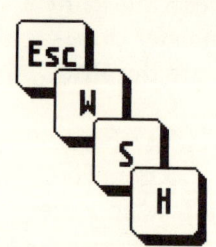

- Press the Esc key and type the letters *WSH*.
- In the At Line selection, type the line number in the active window where you want the new window to split.
- If you want to clear the new window as you split it, answer *Yes* at clear new window.
- Press the Enter key.

Splitting a footnote window from the keyboard. Footnote windows may also be split easily using the keyboard. Here is how to accomplish it:

- If you already have more than one window open, use the F1 key to activate the window in which you plan to open the footnote window.

Using Multiple Text Windows

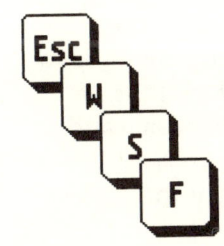

- Press the Esc key and type the letters *WSF*.
- In the At Line selection, type the line number in the active window where you want the new window to split.
- Or press the F1 key and use the arrow keys to select location.
- Press the Enter key.

Closing Windows

You can close windows with either the keyboard routine or directly with your mouse. As always, it's easier to do it with the mouse than through the command menus.

Closing a window from the keyboard. Here's how to close a window from the keyboard:

- Press the Esc key and type the letters *WC*.
- Type the number of the window to be closed.
- Press the Enter key.

Closing a window with the mouse. It's just as easy to close a window with the mouse as it is to open it.

- Move the mouse pointer to the right edge of the window you wish to close.
- When the pointer becomes the splitter box, press both buttons on the mouse. An X will appear in the box.
- When you release both buttons, the window will close.

You can close all but the primary window by moving the pointer to the rightmost borderline and repeating the above procedure until all the windows are gone.

Moving Windows

Once you have windows open, you may decide that you want to move them around onscreen. You can do this either with the command menus or with your mouse.

If you have a mouse, you can easily move many windows to make them smaller or larger. But you cannot reposition the bottom border line onscreen.

199

Chapter 19

Moving one window will generally cause all the other windows to move. The most common reason for moving is to make the active window dominant while you work in it. If this is your intent, consider zooming instead. It's easier and more effective.

Moving windows with the mouse. Probably the easiest way to move windows is with the mouse:

- Put the mouse pointer at the bottom right corner of the window to be moved.
- A symbol will appear that looks like crossed arrows.
- Press either right or left buttons and drag the symbol to the new position for the window.
- When you release the button, the window will move. All the other windows will adjust accordingly.

Moving a window with the menu. When you move a window through the Window Move menu, you move its lower right corner to a different row and column. When you call the menu, the current coordinates will be displayed.

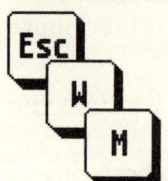

- Press the Esc key and type the letters *WM*.
- Type the number of the window you want to reposition.
- The coordinates of the selected window will be displayed.
- Type the new row number.
- Type the new column number.
- Press the Enter key.

Setting the Window Options

The follow are the display options available through the Window Options menu.

Window number. Specify the window whose options are to be changed. When you call the Window Options menu, the number of the active window will be displayed. You can activate the window you want to change before calling the Window Options menu or you can select a window by typing its number here. This will call up the settings of the particular window.

Outline. *Microsoft Word* has a built-in outlining mode that you can expand or collapse for convenient display. This is where you turn it on. This feature is beyond the scope of this chapter.

Show hidden text. Use this window option to select whether hidden text should be displayed onscreen. When displayed, it's shown as text underlined with dots. When not displayed, hidden text simply disappears. When hidden text is not displayed, it's said to be double-hidden. When double-hidden, text also becomes invisible to global search-and-replace. It is, however, still in the document and will be moved with the text in any cut-and-paste procedure.

Background color. If you have a color monitor, you can change the background color of the text windows. This allows you to customize the appearance of the display to your personal tastes. When the highlight is on this selection, press the F1 key to call the list of window colors. Make your selection from the list with the arrow keys. You may set the background color for each window individually. This provides color coding of the windows by content, to help you keep them straight.

Style bar. Turning on the style bar shifts the display over approximately one-eighth of an inch to make room for the style bar display. This provides an onscreen display of any special style and paragraph tags attached to text in the document. If you're using different formatting options throughout the document, this display can provide a reminder as to what is what. Most people find it convenient to have the style bar visible in each window.

Ruler. Most people find it helpful to have the ruler line on when working with a single document. But if you have multiple windows open, it can be redundant and can take up a line onscreen that could be better used for displaying text. The only time you need it onscreen is when you have to know exactly where text is being positioned by indents or margin changes or when you're setting and using custom tab stops. Otherwise, you may opt to turn it off.

Chapter 19

Changing the defaults. When *Microsoft Word* boots up, it gives the primary text window the default option settings. Any other window you split open will have the same defaults. If this isn't satisfactory, you can change the options for each window individually.

If you change these options for the primary window and then exit from *Microsoft Word* and save the changes, they'll become the new window defaults. Every time you boot up *Microsoft Word*, it'll use them to set up the primary window.

- Press the Esc key and type the letters *WO*.
- At Window Number, type the number of the window whose options you want to change.
- At Outline, the default answer is *No*. Answer *Yes* if you're going to write an outline in the window with *Microsoft Word's* outlining feature.
- At Show Hidden Text, the default answer is *Yes*. Answer *No* to make hidden text disappear from the onscreen display.
- At Background Color, the default is 0. To change it, press the F1 key and select the new color from the list. This only works if you have a color monitor.
- At Style Bar, the default is *No*. Answer *Yes* if you want the style tag symbols to display in the left margin.
- At Ruler, the default is *No*. Answer *Yes* if you want a ruler line displayed at the top of the window.

Using the Transfer Options with Windows

The routine for loading a document file into a secondary window is little different from the method to which you may have become accustomed. Activate the desired window, and then use the standard Transfer Load command.

- Use the mouse or the F1 key to make the window active.
- Press the Esc key and type the letters *TL*.
- If the file is in the logged drive and directory, press the F1 key to call the list and make your selection. If it isn't, then type in the drive and filename.
- Press the Enter key.

Using Multiple Text Windows

Automatic character counting. Whenever you load a file into a window, *Microsoft Word* will automatically execute a count of the characters in that file.

Merging files. The file-merging option is basically what you use to cut and paste very large pieces of reusable text. It can also be used to rejoin the different chapters or parts of a larger document. There are times when it's preferable to merge a file into an empty window, rather than loading it in.

If you're revising a document, you must merge it into a document in order to assign it a new name. Otherwise, when you save it, the revision will overwrite the earlier draft. When you merge a file, the merged document assumes whatever name you give it when you save it.

- Use the mouse or the F1 key to make the window active. 
- Press the Esc key, and type the letters *TM*.
- If the file is in the logged drive and directory, press the F1 key to call the list and make your selection. If it isn't, type in the drive and filename.
- Press the Enter key.

Saving a window. While working with two or more windows, you must be careful and selective about saving them. This is especially true if you have several documents in memory. If you use the macro command Ctrl-F10 to save a file, it'll save whatever window happens to be active. If the wrong window is active, this could be disastrous.

If you're using other documents as a source of boiler-plate text, you probably never want to save them. If you do save them, you may discover later that you have altered them in some way that you didn't intend to be permanent. Just clear the window when you're finished and answer *No* when it asks if you want to save the changes.

- Use the mouse or the F1 key to make the window active.

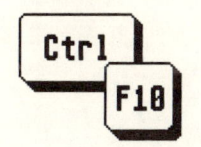

- Hold down the Ctrl key and then press the F10 key.

203

Chapter 19

Deleting files. The main reason for deleting files while working with multiple windows is simply as a housekeeping chore. If you run out of room on an archive disk, you have to delete useless files to make room for the new ones.

Microsoft Word's delete routine will delete files from the currently logged drive and directory. All you have to do is call up the delete menu, display the list, and pick your choice. But if the files to be deleted are on a different drive or directory, you have to log onto that drive with Transfer Options. If you're a new computer user, you probably won't know how to do that. If you're an experienced computer user, you'll undoubtedly find it cumbersome.

It's easier to use the Library Run command to access DOS directly for deleting excess files.

Deleting with the Transfer Delete menu. This routine works best for deleting files from the currently logged drive.

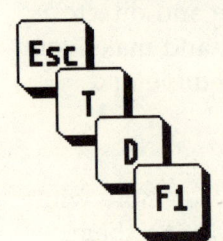

- Press the Esc key and type the letters *TD*.
- Press the F1 key to call the list.
- Use the arrow keys to make your selection.
- Press the Enter key.
- When asked if you're sure, answer *Yes*.

If the files are not in the currently logged drive, then use Transfer Options to log onto another drive. If you don't want to go to the trouble, then use DOS directly to delete the files.

Using DOS. All DOS commands are available to you when you're using *Microsoft Word*. Here's how to issue a DOS command:

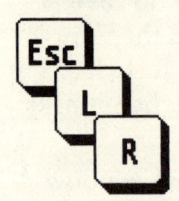

- Press the Esc key and type the letters *LR*.
- Delete the files with DEL or ERASE command. All DOS commands are available to you, including DIR. If you aren't sure of the name of the file you want to delete, use DIR to look at the files on disk.
- Return to *Microsoft Word* by pressing any key at the prompt *Press a key to resume Word*.

Using Multiple Text Windows

Renaming files. The renaming command can be used to change the name of any file in any window. When you call the Transfer Rename menu, it'll display the drive, path, and filename of the file in the currently active window. Before you call the menu, activate the window of the document you wish to rename.

- Use the mouse or the F1 key to make the window active.
- Press the Esc key and type the letters *TR*.
- Take careful note of the current drive and path the file is saved in. You will have to type the drive and path exactly as it appears, changing only the filename.
- Press the Enter key.

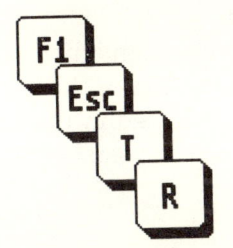

The other use for renaming is as a housekeeping tool. If you want to keep using the same name for the current latest draft, use renaming to change the name of the old version. Or you can use renaming to add or change the filename extensions.

Using the Footnote/Endnote Window

This was saved until last, mainly because its use is built on all the other standard features of multiple window use.

A footnote or endnote window is a special window you can open and use only in conjunction with the footnote or endnote feature of *Microsoft Word*. Whether you print them as footnotes or as endnotes, when you insert a reference note with that feature, the text always goes at the end of the text file. If you are working with a large document, it's inconvenient to jump back and forth in the document every time you insert or revise a reference note.

The reference note window opens directly onto the note text at the end of the file and displays it at the bottom of the screen. You can then jump back and forth from body text to reference notes by pressing the F1 key.

Opening a footnote or endnote window. These are the steps for opening and placing a footnote window at the bottom of your regular text window. The value you must set for the At Line selection refers to the line in the window where

Chapter 19

the top of the footnote window is to be. It has nothing to do with the text in your document.

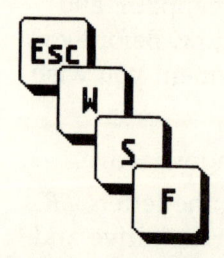

- If you have several window open, it is best to turn on zooming before you open a footnote/endnote window.
- Press the Esc key and type the letters *WSF.*
- Press the F1 key. This makes a highlight appear on the left side of the window.
- Use the cursor keys to place the highlight on the line where you want the top of the footnote window to be. This position will be reflected in the At Line selection.
- Press the Enter key.
- The window will open.

Guidelines for footnote windows. Footnote windows are useful when you need to keep track of your footnotes. The footnote window uses the bottom portion of the main text window, and is separated from the main window by a dotted line across the screen.

When you initially open this footnote window, it will have the same display settings as your main document window. For example: If the main window has a ruler, the footnote window will, too. But you can set the Window Options separately for this window, and have them display as you wish.

Opening this footnote window does not change the location of the text typed into the footnotes/endnotes. They are still being inserted at the end of the document. This special window simply lets you type, edit, and look at the notes without having to jump to them. You can split a footnote window in any text window you have open.

You can cut and paste between footnote/endnote windows, and other windows, with the standard routines. But if you are inserting new reference notes, insert the number first, and then paste into the space it automatically sets aside.

Inserting a reference note. These are the steps for typing a footnote or endnote while using the special footnote window.

Using Multiple Text Windows

- Put the cursor after the last character in the quotation you are referencing.
- Press the Esc key and type the letters *FF*.
- For automatic numbering, press the Enter key.
- For book numbering, type in the correct number and then press Enter key.

• *Microsoft Word* will insert the number as directed, then jump to the footnote window.
• The cursor will be to the right of the footnote number. Just type it in using the correct style and layout. If you want blank lines between reference notes, add them with the Enter key.
• When finished, press the F1 key. This will jump you back to the text window.

Closing footnote window. These are the steps for closing the footnote window when you don't need it anymore.

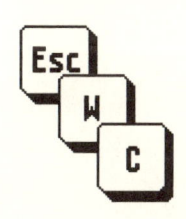

- Use the mouse or the F1 key to activate the window with the footnote/endnote window you want to close.
- Press the Esc key and type the letters *WC*.
- Use the F1 key to put the highlight on the footnote window's number.
- Press the Enter key.

You can use this same routine to close any open window.

Using zooming with footnote/endnote windows. Opening a reference note window has very little effect on using the window zooming feature. You cannot zoom a reference-note window. It is subordinate to a normal text window. You can only zoom in on the main window of which it is a part.

207

Chapter 20
Hyphenating Text

Hyphenation can be used to improve the appearance of your printed documents. If you're printing fully justified text, *Microsoft Word* will insert incremental spaces between the words to make each line exactly the same length. The result will be attractive left and right margins, but some of the words may have unreasonably large spaces between them. One partial solution to this problem is to hyphenate words that fall at the end of each line. This will allow you to print more text on each line and fill in some of those unsightly gaps.

With *Microsoft Word*, you can control hyphenation manually or with an automatic feature. Manual hyphenation gives you the most precise control over your printed lines. Automatic hyphenation is fine for printing documents where precise control is not needed.

Manual Hyphenation

With manual hyphenation, you simply insert a hyphen into the words that fall on the beginning of each line in a paragraph. Then *Microsoft Word* will break off the word at the hyphen and reform the paragraph within its set justification status.

There are three different kinds of hyphens you can insert manually.

Normal hyphen. This will break the line after the hyphen. Use this when you want the hyphen to print whether it breaks the line or not. For example, in the phrase *one-by-one.*

Optional hyphen. Other programs call this a soft hyphen. It will display onscreen, but it won't break the line unless the word falls at the end of a line. If you add or delete enough text to change the alignment of the paragraph, then word-wrap will unbreak the line and put the word

209

Chapter 20

back together again. This is the same kind of hyphen that the autohyphenation routine inserts. If your document has a word you don't want to hyphenate, then manually add an optional hyphen to the end of the word.

Nonbreaking hyphen. This is used to keep a word from breaking during an autohyphenation. If a word falls on a hyphenation point during a rehyphenation, then *Microsoft Word* will break the line in the space before the word. Use this to "take back" a line break after an autohyphenation by replacing the normal or optional hyphen with the nonbreaking type. Some words don't hyphenate well; they lose some of their effectiveness if broken in half during a hyphenation. These might be hyphenated names or phrases. For example, *side-by-side,* or *Sir Sidney Ashton-Tate.*

Inserting a hyphen. Here are the steps for inserting a hyphen:

- To insert a normal hyphen, press the hyphen (-) key.

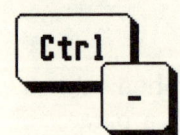

- To insert an optional hyphen, hold down the Ctrl key and press the hyphen key.

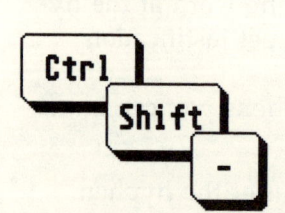

- To insert a nonbreaking hyphen, hold down both the Ctrl key and the Shift key, and then press the hyphen key.

In order to see the optional hyphens, you must have the Options Visible selection set to either Partial or Complete.

Deleting hyphens. All three types of hyphens can be deleted from a document like normal text. Just put the cursor on them and press the Del key. In order to see the Optional Hyphens, you must have the Options Visible selection set to either Partial or Complete.

Using Automatic Hyphenation

Nothing could be simpler to use than the automatic hyphenation. You can hyphenate all or part of any document. Hyphenation will begin at the current cursor location. To hyphenate all of a document, put the cursor at the very beginning of the document. To hyphenate part of a document, place the cursor at the beginning of the section. The last option is to restrict the hyphenation to a specific portion of the file. To take advantage of this option, highlight the section to be hyphenated.

Starting autohyphenation. Here is how to initiate automatic hyphenation:

- Position the cursor or cover the text with the cursor highlight.
- Press the Esc key and type the letters *LH*.
- Set Confirm to *No*.
- Select hyphenate caps Yes or No.
- Press the Enter key.

Confirm hyphen placement. You have the option of making hyphenation a semiautomatic process. When you make this selection, *Microsoft Word* will allow you to make the final decision whether to insert a hyphen at each location. Start the hyphenation as in the steps above, but set Confirm to *Yes*.

- Position the cursor or cover the text with the cursor highlight.
- Press the Esc key and type the letters *LH*.
- Set confirm to *Yes*.
- Select hyphenate caps Yes or No.
- Press the Enter key.
- *Microsoft Word* will begin the hyphenation. When it comes to a candidate location for a hyphen, it will pause with the cursor on the spot where a hyphen is called for.
- You may then accept the hyphenation, alter it, or reject it.
- Accept by pressing the Y key.
- Alter it by using the up- or down-arrow keys to move to alternate hyphenation points; then press the Y key.

Chapter 20

- Alter it by using the up- or down-arrow keys to move to alternate hyphenation points; then press the Y key.
- Reject it by pressing the N key.
- *Microsoft Word* will move to the next hyphenation candidate or the end of the file, whichever comes first.

Pause or stop hyphenation. Here's how to stop or temporarily pause hyphenation:

- You can pause at any point during a hyphenation by pressing the Esc key.
- To resume the hyphenation, press the Y key.

- To stop the hyphenation, press the Esc key a second time.

212

Chapter 21
Numbering Text

The Library Number command will let you automatically number and renumber headings or paragraphs in a *Microsoft Word* text file. This was mainly intended to be used with the Outline mode. But it can be used with any document, and it can be used in conjunction with the autosort feature.

Guidelines for numbering an outline. To number an outline, use the Library Number command to number all headings that do not begin with a hyphen (-), asterisk (*), or bullet (the square bullet is character 254 in the extended character set).

Unless you tell it otherwise, *Microsoft Word* will number outlines following the numbering scheme prescribed in *The Chicago Manual of Style*, published by the University of Chicago Press. That scheme is: Roman numerals first, then capital letters, then Arabic numbers, then lowercase letters.

You can use the progressive or legal numbering system, or you can set the numbering format at each level of heading. You can renumber the entire document or only part of it. The renumbering will begin at the cursor position and move toward the end of the file. You can control the amount of document renumbered by the cursor placement. You can restrict the renumbering to a specific portion of the document by highlighting the section to be renumbered.

Microsoft Word will number only the headings. Body text will not be numbered.

Steps for numbering an entire outline. Here is how to number an outline:

- Put the cursor on the first character of the outline.
- Press the Esc key and type the letters *LN*.
- Select Update.
- Set restart sequence to *Yes*.
- Press the Enter key.

Chapter 21

Numbering with progressive numbers. Progressing numbers offer a viable alternative to outline-style numbers. Here is how to use progressive numbering:

- If you want to use progressive or legal numbering, at the very beginning of the outline to be numbered, type 1 followed by a blank space.
- Put the cursor on the 1.
  - Press the Esc key and type the letters *LN*.
  - Select Update.
  - Set restart sequence to *Yes*.
  - Press the Enter key.

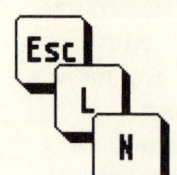

Separate number formats for heading levels. You can set the individual number format for any heading level in order to make that heading level stand out. In the standard outline format, an eighth-level heading will have the same kind of number as the seventh level (lowercase Roman numeral). You can use any numbering format that *Microsoft Word* can recognize.

- Number the entire outline either with the default or with the progressive numbering format.
- If you're in the collapsed viewing mode for outlining, press Shift-F5 to uncollapse the view. (This will take you from *outline organize* mode to *outline edit* mode.) You must be in the normal viewing mode.
- Put the cursor on the first number level you want to renumber.
- Delete the old format, and type in the new number format.
- Put the cursor back on the beginning of that new number format.
  - Press the Esc key and type the letters *LN*.
  - At the Library Number menu, select Update. Set restart sequence to *Yes*.
  - Press the Enter key. *Microsoft Word* will renumber every level of that heading with the new numbering format.

Numbering Text

Renumbering paragraphs. If you number your paragraphs and then cut and paste to rearrange the paragraphs, the paragraph numbering will be inaccurate. There are two ways to correct this. You can manually renumber the paragraphs one by one, deleting the incorrect numbers and typing in the new. Or you can use the automatic renumbering feature of the Library Number command.

- After you finish rearranging the paragraphs with cut and paste, put the cursor back on the first number at the beginning of the document.
  - Press the Esc key and type the letters *LN*.
  - At the Library Number menu, select Update.
  - Then set restart sequence to *Yes*.
  - Press the Enter key.
  - *Microsoft Word* will renumber every paragraph, using the same numbering format already set out in the document.

Removing the numbers. If you have numbered the paragraphs with a standard format that *Microsoft Word* recognizes, you can use the Library Number Remove command to take out the numbers when you are through with them. They can be removed throughout the entire document or from any marked section of text. This eliminates your having to manually delete them one by one.

- Put the cursor at the place where you want the Number Remove to begin. (It will proceed from the cursor position to the end of text.) Or cover the desired portion with the cursor highlight.
  - Press the Esc key and type the letters *LNR*.
  - The restart sequence option has no effect in a number removal.
  - Press the Enter key.

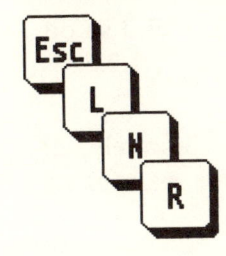

Using Different Numbering Systems

In most cases, it doesn't matter what numbering system you use in your documents or outlines. Personal preference and company policy are the most common determining factors. It would be a good idea to keep your numbering system as simple as possible.

If you're numbering headings in a document that contains numbered lists or tables, besides the normal paragraphs, you must use a numbering system different from that used to number the lists or tables. Otherwise, you stand the risk of accidently renumbering your lists and tables as headings and subheads.

There are two ways to set up a number so *Microsoft Word* will recognize what you type as a number:

- Follow the number with a period and then a blank space.
- Enclose the number between parentheses.

Using progressive numbering. If you're going to reshuffle a document that's divided into sections, subsections, subsubsections, and so on, then use the progressive numbering system. It has also been called legal numbering, because it is so often used in writing contracts where each level of importance must be clearly marked. But it's just as commonly used in technical manuals, especially in government documentation.

Progressive numbering works well with complicated autosorts, because it allows numbering each paragraph according to its relative status in the document.

- Chapters are numbered: 1, 2, 3, 4, 5, 6, and so on.
- Sections are numbered: 1.1, 1.2, 1.3, 2.1, 2.1, 2.3, and so on.
- Subsections are numbered: 1.1.1, 1.1.2, 1.1.3, 1.2.1, 1.2.2, and so on.

The progression of numbers can continue indefinitely, letting you specify every level of your document for rearranging with autosort.

Chapter 22
Checking Spelling

The spelling checker program will check words in either a *Microsoft Word* document, an ASCII file, or an individual word that you type in. These words are compared against the dictionaries stored on disk. You'll only have to correct a misspelling once in any document. The program will "remember" the correction you've made and replace it globally in the document.

Below is a list of some of the things it'll present onscreen for your consideration:

Misspelled words. Words that are actually misspelled.
Suspect words. Words that are not in any of the dictionaries being used for the spelling check. You may ignore these or add them to the personal dictionary.
Repeated words. If you accidently type a word twice, the spelling checker will find it. It's easy for you to notice when both words are on the same line, but if a word is at the right end of one line and the left end of the next line, even a seasoned proofreader might not catch it.
Plural words. The spelling checker may not have plural versions of all the words in its dictionaries, so it may identify a simple plural as a misspelling. You may ignore these or add them to the personal dictionary.
Proper nouns. These are names of people, places, and things. You may ignore them or add them to the personal dictionary.
Jargon. The main dictionary contains few instances of jargon. And the personal dictionary will be virtually empty when you first start using it. If you use jargon in your documents, the spelling checker will stop on every instance it doesn't recognize. Make sure the terms are spelled correctly, and then add them to the personal dictionary. Then the spelling checker will ignore them and no longer will stop on them.
Hidden text. The spelling checker will check hidden text, whether or not it's visible.

Chapter 22

Running a Spelling Check

If you're using *Microsoft Word* on a floppy disk system, it will prompt you to swap in the Dictionary disk before proceeding. When you finish with the spelling check, you must put in the Program disk to continue.

Whenever you run the Library Spell command, *Microsoft Word* automatically saves the text files in the active window. Then it runs the spelling check program. This presents you with the Spell Check menu. There are six options on this menu:

Dictionary. Creates or selects the User Dictionary to use for spelling checks. You can create specialized personal dictionaries for specialized kinds of documents.
Help. Displays reference information for spelling check commands. You can look up information directly on the other menu commands.
Lookup. Will let you check the spelling of an individual word. Just type in the word and press the Enter key.
Options. Sets the options for spelling checks. These are:
  Quick
  Complete
  Ignore capitalization
  Character used to indicate misspellings
  Automatic correction
  Manual correction
Proof. This will start checking the document. When a misspelled or suspect word is found, it'll be presented for correction.
Quit. This will exit from the spelling check and return you to *Microsoft Word*.

Proofing the entire document. Here are the steps to follow in order to proof an entire document:

- Place the cursor at the beginning of the document you wish to spell check.

- Press the Esc key and type the letters *LS*.
- *Microsoft Word* will save the file in the current active window, and then it will present you with the Spelling Check menu. The highlight will always be on the word *Proof*.
- To start the spelling check for the entire document, press the P key.
- When *Microsoft Word* encounters a misspelled or suspect word, that word will be presented for correction. Select from the options on the Proofing menu.
- Unless you select Quit, the Proof will continue through the remainder of the document.
- When the proofing is complete, you'll be returned to *Microsoft Word*.

The Proof menu selections. Here are the options available when proofing:

Add. This will add the suspect word, as-is, to the personal dictionary currently being used.
Correct. This allows you to type a correction from the keyboard. The spelling check will check the spelling of the word you type.
Lookup. This allows you to type a word for the spelling checker to check. When it's finished checking, you'll still be in the Proof menu.
Help. This accesses the help messages for the spelling check.
Ignore. This will leave the suspect word exactly as it is. Use this when you want to leave a word in place but don't want to add it to the personal dictionary.
Mark. This will mark the suspect word with a special character. You can select this character from the Spelling Check main menu.
Options. This lets you choose between a Quick or Complete spelling check and between automatic or manual correction.
Quit. This will abort the spelling check.

Chapter 22

Look up a specific word. To be perfectly frank, this is a very slow way to look up an individual word. You might find it more time-efficient to reach for your dictionary. In the time it takes to use this feature a hundred times, you could drive to a corner bookstore and buy a dictionary.

None of the spelling check program seems to be memory-resident. The entire program appears to be run, and the dictionaries accessed, every time you start the routine.

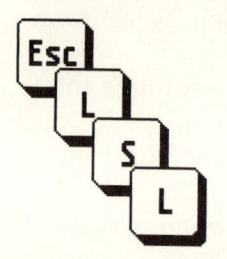

- Press the Esc key and type the letters *LSL*.
- *Microsoft Word* will save the file in the currently active window and then will present you with the Spelling Check Lookup menu.
- Type the word you want to look up.
- Press the Enter key.
- The spelling of the word will be checked against the spell-check dictionaries being used.
- When the spelling check is complete, you may use any of the other spelling check selections.
- When you Quit the spelling check, you will be returned to *Microsoft Word*.

Help with spelling checker. You can get help at any time while running a spelling check.

- At either the Main or the Proofing menu, press the H key to call the Help menu.
- Type the first letter of the feature with which you need help.
- The help messages for that feature will be displayed onscreen, and the help menu will still be active.
- When finished with the Help menu, type *R* for Resume. You'll be returned to whichever menu you were in previously.

The spelling check options. The options on the main Spelling Check menu are used to set up the variations for spelling checks. As mentioned above, these are:

- Quick or Complete
- Ignore capitalization
- Marking character to be used to indicate a misspelled word
- Automatic or manual correction

Quick or Complete. This is used to limit the suggested alternatives. If you choose Quick, the spelling checker will assume that the first two letters of the misspelled word are correct. The search for alternative words will be restricted to the remaining letters of the misspelled word. If you choose Complete, every letter in every word will be used to check for alternative words.

Ignore all caps. This means to ignore words that are typed in all capital letters. Such things might be initials, acronyms, or programming language commands. If you want the check to ignore these, set the option to *Yes*.

Marking character. The spelling checker will mark a word with a character of your choice and then will move on to the next suspect word. Use this when you can't decide what to do about the word and would prefer to handle it during a write-and-edit session. The characters from which you may choose are:

\#
\\
/
%
+
@

Manual or Auto. When you set this to Automatic, the spelling checker will display a list of suggested corrections for the misspelled or suspect words. The list will appear when you choose Correct. Use the arrow keys to make your selection; then press the Enter key.

Removing a word from a dictionary. Sometimes you may add a word to your dictionary and then change your mind. Or you may discover that you misspelled the word.

- Use Transfer Load to open the document file. It'll have the .CMP extension.
- Delete the word or correct the spelling.
- Save the file and exit.

Chapter 22

With the standard or main dictionary, you can only delete the words that have been added to it. You cannot access the other words.

Using the Thesaurus

A *thesaurus* is a list of synonyms. There really isn't much involved in using the thesaurus. You just call it up and use it. Then continue with your write-and-edit session.

Looking up a synonym. The word must be correctly spelled for the synonym finder to be reliable in its search.

- Put the cursor on the word for which you want a synonym.
- Press the Esc key and type the letters *LE*. (You'll notice that, on the Library menu, thesaurus is spelled thEsaurus, which means it's selected by typing *E* rather than *T*, which would select Table.)
- *Wordfinder* will check the selected word against its 220,000-word thesaurus.
- If there are synonyms for the word, they'll appear in a list onscreen.
- Use the arrow keys to move the highlight to the synonym of your choice.
- Press the Enter key to replace the word with its synonym. Use Ctrl-F6 to look up synonyms of a synonym. Or press the Esc key to exit from *Word Finder*.
- When you exit or replace a word, you'll be returned to the place at which you left off in *Microsoft Word*.

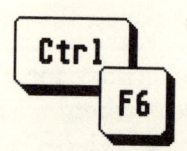

Chapter 23
Generating a Table of Contents

A *table of contents* is a list of the document's contents, organized by chapter, section, subsection, and so on, and it provides the beginning page for each division. This table is, by tradition, found at the front of the document and is used as a cross-reference to help the reader locate general or specific information.

Microsoft Word can generate a table of contents from either embedded table codes in the document or from an outline created with the outline mode.

If you have an outline created already, it's more convenient to use it to generate your table of contents. But it's more flexible to use the table codes. They allow you to create headings different from those in the outline.

Whenever you do a substantive reorganization of a document, as with an autosort, you'll find it simpler to generate a new table of contents rather than cutting and pasting or correcting the old one. This will ensure that the table accurately represents the contents of the document.

Making a table of contents. Here are the steps necessary to make a table of contents:

- If you intend to generate the table of contents from an outline, write the document in the Outline Mode. Of course, this will require you to learn how to use the Outline Mode first. Many people have no need for that tool.
- If you intend to generate the table of contents from table codes, insert those codes as you type the document. This may seem tedious at first, but it quickly will become just another part of writing. When you finish the document, the codes will be in place for you to generate the table of contents. In the long run, you'll find this the most painless approach.
- Load the document into a text window.

Chapter 23

- Run the Library Table command.
- Set up the options on the menu.
- Press the Enter key.
- *Microsoft Word* will generate the table of contents.

Marking the Document for Table of Contents

If you plan to generate the table of contents from an outline, write the document in the Outline Mode. This is simpler than going back and reinserting the outline form after the document is complete. And you'll have the use of the Outline Mode's organizing features. But this, of course, means you must learn how to use the Outline Mode first. Since this is an advanced feature, only passing mention of it has been made in this book.

If you have an outline created already, it would be more convenient to generate your table of contents using the outline, but the table codes are more flexible. They allow you to create headings different from those in the outline.

The parts of a table code entry. Each table of contents entry must have three different parts:

- The table code itself.
- The text that is to appear in the table of contents line.
- An endmark that tells *Microsoft Word* where the end of the entry is. The endmark can be either a semicolon, paragraph mark, or division mark. The most commonly used are the paragraph and the semicolon, in that order.

The entire table code entry must be format-tagged as hidden text. Otherwise it'll print in the document.

Marking the document with table codes. Here's how to insert table codes:

- Make sure Window Options is set to either Partial or Complete.
- Put the cursor on the first character of the heading to be included in the table of contents.

Generating a Table of Contents

- Hold down the Alt key and then press the E key twice. This turns on the Hidden Text tagging.
- Type .C. onto the line.
- Now type a colon (:) for every level of subordination the heading takes. For example, chapters would have no colon, sections would have one colon, subsections would have two colons, and so on. These colons set the level of indention for the headings on the table of contents. One colon equals one indent.
- Hold down the Alt key and then press the space bar twice. This restores the tagging to normal text.
- Repeat the above steps for every heading, subhead, and subsubhead you wish to include in the table of contents.

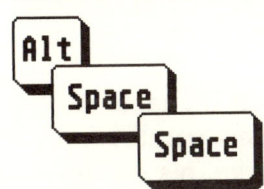

Some shortcuts.

- Save each level of heading table code to a glossary. Then insert each from the glossary instead of typing them. Give them a one-character name, to save yourself a lot of typing. This is the best way to insert the codes if you are going to put them in as you write the document.
- Insert the table code once, then go through the document to each corresponding level of heading, and use the repeat command key F4 to insert the code.
- Use the supplied macro table of contents_entry.mac to insert the table codes and endmarks around the heading.

Special treatment required. If your headings contain colons, semicolons, or quotation marks, they'll need special treatment. The table of contents generation routine uses these punctuation marks as coding symbols.

- If you need to use the marks in the normal way, enclose the entire heading entry in quotation marks, as in .c."Paducah: City or City-State?".

225

Chapter 23

- If your heading contains quotation marks used normally, then you must use two quotation marks for every normal mark you want to print, as in .c." " "Murder," " she wrote.".

If you leave off these enclosing quotation marks, it will ruin the generated table of contents.

Generating the Table of Contents

When you execute the Library Table command, it'll call up the table of contents menu. From there you can set the options, and then you can set the routine in motion. It will repaginate the document, compile a sequential list of the entries, and assign each a page number.

When it does this, *Microsoft Word* will put the table of contents at the end of your document. It'll be separated from the rest of the document with a division mark. This will let you tag formatting exclusively to the table of contents.

If you have footnote/endnote text at the end of your document, the table of contents will be inserted between the body of the document and the footnote/endnote text.

As the first line of the table, *Microsoft Word* will insert the hidden text *.Begin Table C*. As the last line of the table, *Microsoft Word* will insert *End Table C*. Leave these lines in your document. They are used to identify the table so you can update it later.

It's a good idea to cut and paste this table of contents to a file of its own. Then you can work with the table and print it without having to load its respective document. If you want to print it with the document, you'll have to move it to the beginning of the document anyway.

Running the generation routine. Here are the steps necessary to actually generate the table of contents:

- Load the document into a text window.
- Call the Window Options menu and make sure that Show Hidden Text is set to *No*. Then press the Enter key.

Generating a Table of Contents

- Press the Esc key and type the letters *LT*.
- Select either Outline or Codes.
- Set the other options as you want them.
- Press the Enter key.
- The routine will look for an existing table of contents. If it finds one, you must tell it to overwrite the existing table, or the routine will abort.
- Depending on the size of the document, it'll take several minutes for the table to be generated. When complete, *Microsoft Word* will move the cursor to it.

Formatting the Table of Contents

There are two ways you can control how the table of contents will print. The first way is with the options on the table of contents menu. This will control several factors about how *Microsoft Word* sets up the table as it's generated.

The second way is use normal formatting commands after the table has been completed. It's normal text, and you can attach any format tags you want.

The Table menu options. Below are the details of the options available to you on the Table menu.

Outline or Codes. You can generate a Table of Contents from either an outline you have created with the outline mode or from embedded table codes in the document. Set this option to the method you're using.

Index code. The default character for table codes is the capital letter C. You can change this to another character, but this is not recommended. Changing it in one file will require that you either change it in all your files or make a record of which files use what index code character. It's simpler to stick with the default.

Page numbers. Decide whether you want page numbers to be automatically included in the table of contents.

Entry/page number separated by. The default separator between the end of the table of contents entry and its page number is the standard tab. You can change this prior to generating the file and can substitute other characters instead of blank tabs. Type a period, a series of periods

227

(...), a hyphen, or other character to lead you across the page to the numbers. You are allowed up to 256 characters.

Indent each level. The default indention for each level of heading is .4 inch per colon in the table code. You can type any practical value, in any of the measurement standards that *Microsoft Word* can recognize.

Use a style sheet. If you have a style sheet tagged to the document or division, you decide here whether you want the table of contents generator to use that style sheet's special format tagging.

Formatting the table after you generate it. The generated table of contents is just like any other text. You can format it and lay it out any way you want to.

You can move the page-number column by setting up tabs to put the numbers where you want them. You can also use tabs to insert leading characters between the ends of each table entry and its corresponding page number.

It's very common to number the pages of a table of contents with lowercase Roman numerals. *Microsoft Word* can do this for you. Use the Format Division Page-numbers command to tell *Microsoft Word* to number the pages with lowercase numerals.

Chapter 24
Generating an Index from a Document

An *index* is an alphabetized listing of topics found in a document. Accompanying each topic is a list of the pages where that topic is discussed.

Index codes are embedded in the body of the document. These codes are tagged as hidden text. This will keep them from being printed in the hardcopy of the document.

The types of things you include as index codes are very important to the usefulness of the index. For openers, you may want to include:

- Headings and subheads
- Any special terms used in the document
- The main and supporting subjects of the document
- Abbreviations and acronyms
- Synonyms
- Inverted phrases

You should update the index anytime after revising and reorganizing the document. There's nothing more frustrating than using an index to look up something, and finding that the information isn't where the index said it would be.

The index will be inserted at the end of the document. If the document already has a table of contents, the index will be below it, after a division mark. This will let you apply formatting to the index that does not affect the rest of the document.

Microsoft Word will insert the hidden text *.Begin index.* as the first line of the index. And it will insert *.End Index.* as the last line of the index. Leave this hidden text in place. This tells *Microsoft Word* where the index begins and ends, in the event that you update it.

Chapter 24

Steps to generating an index. Here's how to actually generate an index:

- Write the document.
- Insert the index codes.
- Run the Library Index command.
- Format the index any way you want it to print.

Inserting Index Codes and Entries

Every index code entry has three parts:

- The index code itself, .i., formatted as hidden text. This tells *Microsoft Word* where the index entry begins.
- The text that will print in the index. This is usually a key word or phrase. Keep it short.
- An endmark that tells *Microsoft Word* where the end of the entry is. If you forget an endmark, *Microsoft Word* will include everything up to the next index code as a part of the index. The endmark must also be tagged as hidden text.

Inserting index codes. You can mark existing text as entries for the index, or you can type in all new code lines. The latter is the most positive way of putting your codes in the document

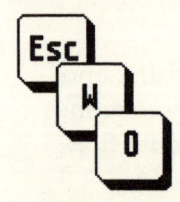

- Press the Esc key and type the letters *WO*. Set Show Hidden Text to *Yes*. Press the Enter key.
- Put the cursor at the position where you want to insert an index code.

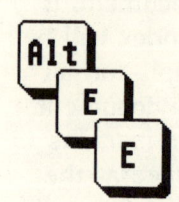

- Hold down the Alt key and then press the E key twice. This turns on the hidden text tagging.

Generating an Index from a Document

- Type *.i.*
- You can insert tabs for subentries by typing a colon immediately after the index code. Type one colon for each indention.
- Now type the entry for the index. Keep it short and simple. Keep a log of your index entries as you type them. It's very important to be consistent with them throughout the document. Changing the spelling, or even the capitalization, can result in two or more entries for the same category.
- Press the Enter key. This will insert a carriage return tagged as hidden text. The entire entry must be tagged as hidden text. This will keep the entry from printing in the document.
- Hold down the Alt key and then press the space bar twice. This turns off the hidden text tagging.
- Repeat the steps above for every index code in the document.

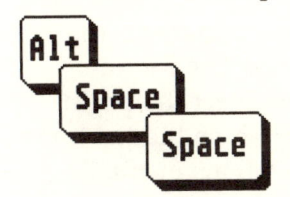

Shortcuts for inserting index codes. Here are a few time-savers for index-generation:

- Save each level of index code to a glossary. Then insert each from the glossary instead of typing them. Give them a one-character name, to save yourself a lot of typing. This is the best way to insert the codes if you're going to put them in as you write the document. If you write similar documents, you may be able to use the same set of code glossaries over and over again.
- Insert the index code once; then go through the document to each corresponding level of index entry and use the repeat command key F4 to insert the code.
- Use the supplied macro index_entry.mac to insert the index codes and endmarks around the index entry.

Special treatment required. If your index entries contain colons, semicolons, or quotation marks, they'll need some special treatment. The Index generation routine uses them as coding symbols.

231

Chapter 24

- If you need to use the marks in the normal way, then enclose the entire index entry entry in quotation marks, as in .i."Breezewood: City of Motels".
- If your index entry contains quotation marks used normally, then you must use two quotation marks for every normal mark you want to print, as in .i." " "Worthless" " education".

If you leave off these quotation marks, your index will be ruined. *Microsoft Word* will include everything up to the next index code.

Compiling the Index

After you've inserted the index codes in the document, the next step is to compile or generate the index. The routine repaginates the document. Hidden text can effect the pagination if it's displayed. So you need to double-hide hidden text by turning off its display at the Window Options menu.

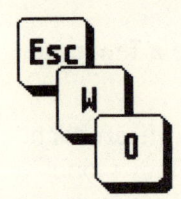

- Load the document into a text window.
- Call the Window Options menu and make sure that Show Hidden Text is set to *No*. Then press the Enter key.

- Press the Esc key and type the letters *LI*.
- Set the options as you want them.
- Press the Enter key.
- The routine will look for an existing index. If it finds one, you must tell it to overwrite the existing index, or the routine will abort.
- Depending on the size of the document, it'll take several minutes for the index to be generated. When the process is complete, *Microsoft Word* will move the cursor to the index.
- The index will be inserted at the end of the document. If the document already has a table of contents, the index will be below it, after a division mark. This will let you apply formatting to the index that does not effect the rest of the document.

Formatting the Index for Printing

There are two ways to control how the index will print. The first way is with the options on the index menu. This will control several factors about how *Microsoft Word* sets up the index as it's generated.

The second way is after the index has been completed. The index is normal text, and you can attach any format tags you want.

The Index menu options. Below are the details of the options available to you on the Index menu.

Entry/page # separated by. The default separator between the end of the index code entry, and its page numbers, is the comma. You can change this before generating the file and can substitute any other character you prefer.

Cap main entries. If *Yes* is selected, *Microsoft Word* will automatically capitalize the main entries in the index.

Indent each level. The default indention for each level of indexing is .2 inch per colon in the index code. You can type in any practical size, using any of the measurement standards that *Microsoft Word* recognizes.

Use style sheet. If you have a style sheet tagged to the document or division, you decide here whether you want the index compiler to use that style sheet's special format tagging.

Formatting the index after you generate it. The generated index is just like any other text. You can format it and lay it out any way you want. You can move the page number column by setting up tabs to put the numbers where you want them. You can also use tabs to insert leading characters between the ends of each index entry and its corresponding page number.

It's very common to number the pages of a Index with lowercase Roman numeral. You can have *Microsoft Word* do this for you. Use the Format Division Page-numbers command to tell *Microsoft Word* to number the pages with lowercase Roman numerals.

You can make a two-column index with the Format Division Layout command. At that menu, set the number of columns to 2.

Chapter 25
Using and Making Style Sheets

Style sheets aren't intended for use by the first-time user. They're meant to be a time-saver for the professional word processor—a secretary, clerk, or staff writer. Style sheets help professional users format entire standardized documents to a preset layout. But anyone can learn to use style sheets for setting up letters and other documents to a preset format.

Style sheets are a formatting aid for writing and editing with *Microsoft Word*. They're easy to use, but they can be difficult for the first-time user to understand, especially someone who has been trying to use the factory documentation from Microsoft. Style sheets are an advanced feature, because their use is built on most of the basic writing, editing, and formatting features of *Microsoft Word*.

Microsoft Word comes with several standard style sheets on disk. If you are working in an office environment, there may be many other style sheets on disk written specifically for your office or company needs. This manual cannot describe them, nor can it tell you how to use them.

Understanding Style Sheets

This chapter is written to give you a clear understanding of style sheets. But it can't begin from scratch and explain all the preceding features and options on which style sheets are based. That would require summarizing this entire book. This chapter presumes that you already have learned the basic terminology and that you know how to use all of the basic features. Without this basic knowledge of *Microsoft Word*, style sheets won't make any sense to you.

Chapter 25

If you're a proficient user of *Microsoft Word*, the information that follows can help you understand what style sheets are so you may apply them to your basic word processing. It will also teach you how to create and edit your own style sheets.

Defining Terms

First you must get the terms straight. The factory documentation for *Microsoft Word* uses the term *styles* three different ways. It refers to a style sheet, to the macro formatting commands on the style sheet, and to using the macros and style sheets to do the formatting.

In order to avoid confusion, this manual uses a separate term for each of those things. These terms are:

- Style Sheet. The macro file of formatting commands.
- Style Tag. An individual formatting macro.
- Alt Command. The command used to execute a style tag.

What is a Style Sheet?

A *style sheet* is nothing more than a set of macros used to format a document. In this case, a *macro* is a formatting command, or a string of formatting commands, you can execute with a few keystrokes (instead of having to work through the command menus). You can use the six style sheets that came with *Microsoft Word*, or you can write your own to meet your special needs.

Each style sheet, with its set of macros, is kept in a distinct file of its own. This macro file may be attached to a document, and its commands will then load into resident memory every time you load that document into a text window. The formatting commands are assigned to specific keys, and you execute them by typing those keys.

The essence of using macros is the speed and convenience they offer. The convenience lies in the fact that you can define each macro to do exactly what you want it to do. You can put together almost any combination of the different kinds of *Microsoft Word* formatting. Once defined, the commands can be issued as one.

What Are Style Tags?

Each style tag is a defined macro for controlling the layout or format of text. There are three basic kinds of style tags. Each style sheet is usually made up of a combination of each of these different style tags.

Character Tags. These are style tags with instructions that set up the character formatting of text either as you type it or afterward. These instructions include all the features and options on the Format Character menu.

Paragraphs Tags. These are style tags that set up the formatting of paragraphs either as you type them or afterward. These instructions include all the features and options on the Format Paragraph menu. A paragraph tag can also contain character format instructions.

Divisions Tags. These are style tags with instructions that set up the page layout in an entire document or within a document division. These instructions include all the features and options on the Format Division menu. A division tag can also contain character and paragraph formatting instructions.

Every style sheet has some macros or style tags that are automatic in that they affect the document as soon as the style sheet is attached to it. When you attach or change the style sheet, you'll see these automatic tags reshape the document.

The remainder of these macros must be deliberately tagged to selected text. There are two different ways you can do this:

- With the options on the Format style sheet menu.
- With Alt Commands.

For What Are Style Sheets Used?

The style sheet is meant to be a shortcut feature. It will allow you to set up a special-purpose style and layout for a document or a division in a document without having to format each paragraph and page individually.

Two of the style sheets that come with *Microsoft Word* are specifically for writing and formatting letters. They use the

Chapter 25

standard full-block and semiblock layouts recommended by *The Chicago Manual of Style*. Just attach either style sheet to the letter you're writing. Then use the Alt Commands to assign the style tags to the parts of the letter as you type it. You won't have to go through any of the Format command menus.

You can use the standard style sheets that come with *Microsoft Word*. Or you can use the write-and-edit features of the Gallery menu to make up your own style sheets. When you write your own style sheets, you can make up one for any kind of layout you may need to print any style or purpose document.

Using style sheets is easy. Writing them is a only a bit more complicated. But if you write many standardized documents, or documents with complicated formatting and layouts, then it's worth the time it takes to write a dedicated style sheet for each of those documents.

If you know how to tag text with the Format menu commands, you already know most of the concepts that underlie style sheets' use. In fact, if you have already formatted a paragraph or division, you can reuse that exact formatting by telling *Microsoft Word* to copy or record it into a style sheet.

Two Menus That Control Style Sheets

Microsoft Word has two menus that control the style sheets. They are only described briefly in this overview. Later in the chapter, there's a section detailing each of them.

The Format Style Sheet menu. With this menu, you can attach a style sheet to a document. Once the style sheet is attached to the text file, you can use the other options on the menu to tag the macros controlling Character, Paragraph, and Division formatting onto the text in the document. The last option on the Format Style Sheet menu lets you record a new style tag.

The Gallery menu. The second menu for controlling style sheets is the Gallery menu. When you call the Gallery, it'll automatically display the style sheet currently attached to the document in the active window. Onscreen will be the list of the style tags of that style sheet, with their formatting instructions clearly revealed. You can attach a style sheet to a

Using and Making Style Sheets

document with the Gallery menu. But the Gallery menu's main purposes are:

- To let you look at the contents of the style sheets.
- To let you create and edit style sheets of your own.

Using the Format Style Sheet Menu

The Format Style Sheet menu has five different options for working with style sheets.

Attach. This is the command to join a style sheet to a document by copying it from disk to the document in the active window.

Character. This command lets you select a specific character style tag from a list and apply it to selected text in your document.

Paragraph. This command lets you select a specific paragraph style tag from a list and then apply it to selected paragraphs in your document.

Division. This command lets you select a specific division tag from a list and then apply it to selected pages or divisions in your document.

Record. This command lets you record a new style tag of any of the three types. You use existing text as a template and then add that tag to the currently attached style sheet. When you exit from *Microsoft Word*, you'll have the option of saving this addition to the style sheet or of letting it erase.

Attaching a Style Sheet to a document. The steps below presume that you have run *Microsoft Word* and have either loaded a text file into a window or are creating a new one. You can attach a style sheet to an empty document, to an existing one for reformatting, or to one that you have just begun.

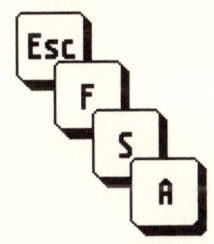

- Press the Esc key and then type the letters *FSA*.
- Press the F1 key to call the list of style sheets.
- Use the arrow keys to move the highlight to your choice.
- Press the Enter key.

239

Chapter 25

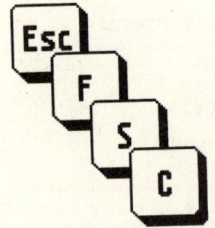

Using a character style tag. Here are the steps for using a character style tag:

- Put the cursor highlight over the text to be formatted with the style tag.
- Press the Esc key and then type the letters *FSC*.
- Press the F1 key to call the list of character style tags for the currently attached style sheet.
- Use the arrow keys to move the highlight to your choice.
- Press the Enter key.

Using a paragraph style tag. Here are the steps for using a paragraph style tag:

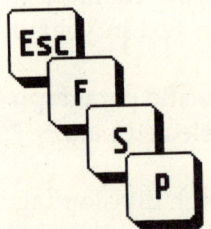

- Put the cursor in the paragraph to be tagged. If tagging multiple paragraphs, put the cursor highlight over all the paragraphs to be formatted with the style tag.
- Press the Esc key and then type the letters *FSP*.
- Press the F1 key to call the list of paragraph style tags for the currently attached style sheet.
- Use the arrow keys to move the highlight to your choice.
- Press the Enter key.

Using a division style tag. Use the following steps to incorporate a division style tag:

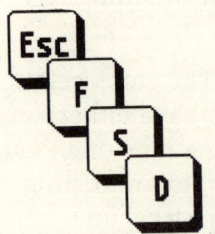

- Put the cursor in the division to be tagged. If tagging multiple divisions, put the cursor highlight over all the divisions to be formatted with the style tag.
- Press the Esc key and then type the letters *FSD*.
- Press the F1 key to call the list of division style tags for the currently attached style sheet.
- Use the arrow keys to move the highlight to your choice.
- Press the Enter key.

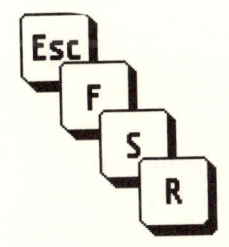

Using and Making Style Sheets

- Put the cursor highlight over the text to be used as the template for your new style tag.
- Press the Esc key and then type the letters *FSR*.
- The Format Style Sheet Record menu will appear at the bottom of the text window.
- The highlight is on Keycode. Type in a two-letter code as a name for the new style tag. It can be any keycode not already used in the current style sheet. But do not begin it with the letter X.
- Use the left-arrow key to move the highlight to Usage. Type the first letter of the kind of style tag you're creating.
- Use the down-arrow key to move the highlight to Remark. In all capitals, type in a short remark that says what the style tag does specifically. You are allowed up to 28 characters, including blank spaces.
- *Microsoft Word* will suggest a variant based on the kind of text marked with the cursor highlight. You can accept that suggested variant or use another. If you want to change the variant, use the left-arrow key to move to it. Press the F1 key to call the list of variants, and use the arrow keys to make your selection.
- You can use the Tab key to go back to any selection to make changes or corrections.
- When you have the style tag correctly identified, press the Enter key to record it.

Writing a new style tag from scratch. The Format Style Sheet Record command only lets you use existing text as a template for a new style tag. But you can write a new one from scratch with the Gallery menu. You can also edit an existing style tag and style sheet through that menu. To learn how to do this, see the section titled "Using the Gallery Menu."

Using *Microsoft Word's* Style Sheets

Below is a list of the style sheets that come with *Microsoft Word*. Just attach them to your documents and use them as directed.

241

Chapter 25

NORMAL.STY. Microsoft speaks of this style sheet as though it were actually a file on disk. In fact, it clearly states that it is to be found on the Utilities disk. But there is no NORMAL.STY style sheet for you to call up and view. This writer has versions of *Microsoft Word* all the way back to release 1.5, and they're not listed on any of those Utility disks. The NORMAL.STY style sheet is simply the set of default values that *Microsoft Word* boots up with and automatically assigns to every window opened. It has a set of style tags that you can neither view nor change. These "normal" tags can still be applied to your text even if you have another style sheet attached to your document.

FULL.STY. This style sheet is used for writing full-block business letters. It contains 13 style tags that will allow you to format and type a standard business letter. The tags determine position of letterhead, inside address, date, and salutation. They also preset the line spacing, font and font size, page size, and margins.

SEMI.STY. This style sheet is used for writing and formatting semiblock business and personal letters, for the times when you don't need the formality of the full standard. The style sheet also contains 13 style tags. They are very similar to those in FULL.STY, but they don't produce a letter as rigidly structured.

SIDEBY.STY. This style sheet is used for aligning related paragraphs for printing side by side. It contains five style tags for setting up your documents in either two- or three-column side-by-side format. The full use of this style sheet is discussed in the chapter about formatting paragraphs.

SAMPLE.STY. This style sheet contains a broad sampling of general-purpose style tags. You can attach the entire style sheet to a document or use its contents as a resource when you are making up new style sheets. The same can be done with any of the style tags in the other style sheets.

OUTLINE.STY. This is the style sheet you attach to a new document when you want to write and view it with the special outlining mode. This will allow you to tag headings, and their accompanying text, to display in either normal text view or in the outline view, where sections and subsections are indented.

Using a Style Sheet

There are two steps to using a style sheet:

- Attach the style sheet to the document or division in a document.
- Apply the style tags to specific text within the document.

These can both be accomplished through the Format Style Sheet menu. Or, once the style sheet is attached to the document, you can apply the style tags with Alt commands.

Attaching a Style Sheet to a document. The steps below presume that you have run *Microsoft Word* and have either loaded a text file into a window or are creating a new one. You can attach a style sheet to an empty document, to an existing one for reformatting, or to one that you have just begun.

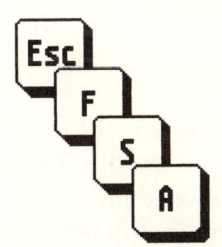

- Press the Esc key and then type the letters *FSA*.
- Press the F1 key to call the list of style sheets.
- Use the arrow keys to move the highlight to your choice.
- Press the Enter key.

Changing Style Sheets. To change the style sheet, simply attach another one to the document or division on which you're working. The new style sheet will replace the old one.

If you change the style sheets attached to documents, it can be as interesting as changing canoes in midstream. You can radically change the format and layout of a document by attaching a different style sheet to it. This is especially true if the new style sheet has different style tags that share the same name as ones in the previous style sheet.

Tagging text with the Format Style Sheet menu. When you have a style sheet attached to a document or to a division within a document, you can apply style tags through the Format Style Sheet menu. This is slower than using the Alt Commands, but it accomplishes the same end.

243

Chapter 25

- Put the cursor highlight over the text to be tagged.
- Press the Esc key and then type the letters *FS*.
- Type the first letter (*C, P,* or *D*) of the kind of style tag you want to select.
- Press the F1 key to call the list of style tags.
- Use the arrow keys to make your selection.
- Press the Enter key.

Tagging text with Alt commands. Once you have attached a style sheet to a document or to a division within a document, you'll use Alt commands to tag the text with style sheet formatting.

- Put the cursor highlight over the text you want to format tag.
- Hold down the Alt key and then type the letter(s) of the style tag you want to use.

The style tags vary from style sheet to style sheet, as do the Alt commands. You must know them for each style sheet you're using.

The letters or numbers typed while holding down the Alt key are simply the keystroke sequence or code assigned to the individual style tags. Like a filename, the keycodes identify the tags so *Microsoft Word* can apply their formatting instructions to the selected text.

You can find these keycodes by viewing the style sheet through the Gallery menu. They will be the letters and numbers in the second column of the onscreen style sheet display. You can also print the entire style sheet and keep it handy as a reference.

This chapter includes print-outs and command summaries of the style sheets provided by Microsoft.

Detaching a style tag from a paragraph. There are two ways of removing style tags from paragraphs in a document.

- Use the respective Format menus, and undo the formatting.
- Use a direct command to restore the paragraph to plain text that has not been formatted.

Using and Making Style Sheets

- Put the cursor in the individual paragraph. If you're undoing several paragraphs, you can cover them all with the cursor highlight.
- Hold down the Alt key and then type the letter *P*.

If you have an alternate style sheet attached, you must type *XP*.

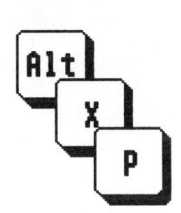

You should be careful not to use this command without thinking ahead. It will remove all of the paragraph formatting from the marked paragraphs. If you only want to remove part of the paragraph tagging, then use the Format Paragraph menu.

Microsoft Word's Standard Style Sheets

What follows is a full explanation of the Alt commands associated with the style sheets provided with *Microsoft Word*.

Table 25-1. Alt Command Summary of SAMPLE.STY

Alt Command	Meaning
NL	Numbered list
TI	Title
SH	Subhead
LE	List entry
SP	Standard paragraph
RH	Running head
L1	Left side-by-side
R1	Right side-by-side
H1	Head, level one
H2	Head, level two
H3	Head, level three

Table 25-2. Alt Command Summary of SIDEBY.STY

Alt Command	Meaning
2L	Left column in two-column side-by-side
2R	Right column in two-column side-by-side
3L	Left column in three-column side-by-side
3C	Center column in three-column side-by-side
3R	Right column in three-column side-by-side

Chapter 25

Table 25-3. Alt Command Summary of SEMI.STY

Alt Command	Meaning
S/	Semiblock letter, 6-inch width
LH	Adjustable letterhead space
RA	Return name, address
DA	Date
IA	Inside address (Mr. Jim Smith)
SA	Salutation (Dear . . .)
SP	Standard paragraph
CL	Complimentary closing (Sincerely)
NA	Author's name (below signature)
TI	Author's title (after name)
RI	Ref initials, enclosures, cc
UC	Underlined

Table 25-4. Alt Command Summary of FULL.STY

Alt Command	Meaning
S/	Full block letter, 6-inch width
LH	Adjustable letterhead space
RA	Return name, address
DA	Date
IA	Inside address (Mr. Jim Smith)
SA	Salutation (Dear . . .)
SP	Standard paragraph
CL	Complimentary closing (Sincerely)
NA	Author's name (below signature)
TI	Author's title (after name)
RI	Ref initials, enclosures, cc
UC	Underlined

Table 25-5. Alt Command Summary of OUTLINE.STY

Alt Command	Meaning
S/	Outline style sheet, 6-inch width
1	Heading level one
2	Heading level two
3	Heading level three
4	Heading level four
5	Heading level five
6	Heading level six
7	Heading level seven

Using the Gallery Menu

Microsoft Word has a special menu you can use to view and revise a style sheet. This is called the *Gallery menu.* This menu works just like any other menu in the program.

The Gallery menu is separate from the write-and-edit mode. Thus, anything you do while at that menu does not automatically affect formatting in the document on which you're working. Selecting Transfer and then Load allows you to display a style sheet's contents onscreen. Once displayed, you may look at the formatting in the style sheet and make changes, if you wish.

When through looking at a style sheet, you can load another or exit from the Gallery menu. *Microsoft Word* will not attach the style sheet unless you specifically tell it to do so at the time you exit. You can look at any or all of the style sheets and make changes without modifying either your document or the style sheet currently attached to it.

Understanding the Gallery Menu

The Gallery menu works like any other menu called from the command bar. You can select from its options with a mouse or by typing the first letter of the submenus listed on it.

The Gallery menu has two modes of its own:

- The selection mode
- The revision mode

While in the selection mode, the arrow keys will move the highlight from style tag to style tag. While in the revision mode, you can edit and revise the formatting instructions in the highlighted style tag.

The Esc key is used to toggle between the selection mode and the revision mode. If you're trying to move the highlight to a different style tag and the arrow keys don't work, press the Esc key and try again.

In this menu, the Esc key also works as a universal abort command. It'll let you escape or abort from any submenu function without making any changes. But it returns you to the Gallery menu instead of to the command bar or the write-and-edit mode.

Chapter 25

The Gallery menu has three main purposes:

- Displaying the instructions in a style sheet.
- Editing a existing style sheet.
- Writing a new style sheet.

Displaying the contents of a style sheet. When you call the Gallery, it automatically will display the style sheet currently attached to the document in the active window. You'll see the list of the style tags of that style sheet onscreen, with their formatting instructions clearly revealed.

If the current style sheet is not the one you want to look at, you can load another into the window to examine.

You can attach a style sheet to a document with the Gallery menu when you've finished editing it or when you've determined it's the one you want to use.

If you don't want to edit or attach that style sheet, you can load another one to examine or edit.

Writing and Editing Style Sheets and Style Tags

Microsoft intended that you use an existing style sheet as a template for creating your new style sheets. You will write a new style sheet by loading an existing one into memory, editing it to fit your purposes, and then saving it under a different name. You can modify the style sheet already attached to your document, or you may load another from the list. The steps below are for loading a style sheet and then modifying it.

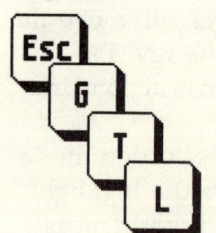

- Press the Esc key and type *GTL*.
- Press the F1 key to call the list of style sheets.
- Use the arrow keys to move the highlight to your choice, and then press the Enter key.
- The selected style sheet will display onscreen. You may now make any changes to any style tag by moving the highlight to it and then using the submenus on the Gallery menu. Insert new tags where you want them. Delete any tags you do not want.
- When you are finished making changes, return to the Gallery menu.

Using and Making Style Sheets

- Type the letters *TS*.
- Now type the name for the new style sheet.
- Press the Enter key.

Microsoft Word will save the altered version to the new name and will leave the original version unchanged. In this way, you can build your own archive of special-purpose style sheets dedicated to the needs of your office, department, or business. Remember, you can always go back and modify any style sheet you have made.

Avoid tag name duplication. When you create a new style sheet by editing its style tags, it is a good idea to rename each altered style tag. In this way, you can avoid name duplication, giving the tag a name that more closely reflects its formatting function.

If you have a tag name on one style sheet duplicated in other style sheets, you won't be able to merge or attach that style sheet to documents already formatted with any of those other style sheets. The duplicate-named style tags in the style sheet being attached or merged will overwrite the tags with the same name already tagged to the document. That will change the formatting of the text.

Changing a style tag's name. Here are the steps to change the name of a style tag:

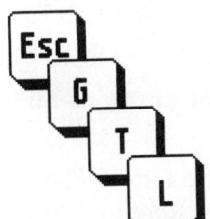

- Press the Esc key and type the letters *GTL*.
- Press the F1 key to call the list of style sheets.
- Use the arrow keys to move the highlight to your choice and then press the Enter key.
- The selected style sheet will display onscreen. Use the arrow keys to move to the tag you want to change and rename. Make the changes you want.
- At the Gallery menu, type the letter *N* (Name).
- The Gallery Name menu will appear, with the current keycode name of the style tag in highlight. Type in the new keycode. Do not begin it with *X*. Other than that, it can be any 1–2 letter combination you want. If possible, make it

249

Chapter 25

something that reflects the purpose of the style tag. To escape without changing the name, press the Esc key.
- After typing the new tag name, use the down-arrow key to move to Remark. Turn on the Caps Lock and type in a new remark that best describes the new function of the altered style tag. You are allowed up to 28 characters. Keep your remark simple and to the point.
- Press the Enter key.

Different ways to write new style tags. You can make a new style tag at any time while *Microsoft Word* is running. But just making up the new tag does not apply its format instructions to the text. That is done with an Alt command.

There are three different ways to create new style tags.

By Example. When you create a style by example, you select text that has the format you want to use again and tell *Microsoft Word* to record that format combination.
From Scratch. You can use the Gallery Insert command to create a new style tag from scratch. Just give it a name and use the Gallery Format menus to assign its particular formatting instructions.
From an Existing Tag. You can copy an existing style tag to the scrap, insert it with the Ins key, then modify it with the Gallery Format menus.

Making a style tag by example. Here are the steps to follow in order to create a style tag by example:

- Put the cursor highlight over the text you want to use as an example for creating a new style tag.
- Press the Esc key and type the letters *FSR*, to call the Format Style Sheet Record menu. (You can accomplish the same thing by using Alt-F10.)
- The highlight will be on Keycode. Type in the 1–2 letter name for the new style tag. (Do not begin it with an X.)
- Use the right-arrow key to move to Usage. Type the first letter of the type style tag you are creating.
- Use the down-arrow key to move to Remark. In all capital

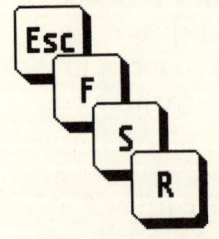

Using and Making Style Sheets

letters, type a remark to identify the function of the style tag. You are allowed up to 28 characters, including spaces.
- You don't need to change the variant, as that is being determined by the text you're using as the example. But if you do want to change it, use the arrow keys to move to it and then press the F1 key to call the list and make your selection. If you attempt to change the variant, *Microsoft Word* will require you to authorize overwriting the existing variant setting.
- You can go back and change anything if it is incorrect. When ready to record the new style tag, press the Enter key.
- If you have the style bar toggled on, you'll see the new tag name appear onscreen.
- Save the style sheet.

Guidelines for style tags by example. If you have a complicated set of format instructions used over and over again, you can record them as a style tag and execute them with one or two keystrokes. The formatted text serves as a template or stencil for the new style tag.

This is accomplished by marking the example text with the cursor highlight and then using the Format Style Sheet Record command. That menu is accessed from the main command bar instead of through the Gallery menu.

Character Tagging. The recording procedure uses the first character in a marked block of text as the example for the character format to be recorded.

Paragraph Tagging. The recording procedure uses the format instructions of the first paragraph in the marked block of text. If all the characters in the marked block have the same format, then that will be used as the tag format.

Division Tagging. The recording procedure uses the division format instructions of the first division in the text you have marked. It doesn't matter if you mark text across a division boundary. If you want specific division formatting to be recorded as a style tag, you must mark it individually.

Making a style tag from scratch. You can make a new style tag from scratch by using the Gallery Insert command. With that command, define the tag name (its keycode, usage,

251

Chapter 25

variant, and remark) as you insert it. Once it is inserted, you'll set up its formatting by using the four Gallery Format menus.

Inserting the new style tag. The first part of creating a new style tag is to insert a blank tag into the style sheet. You can insert a new style tag anywhere in any style sheet, whether it is brand new or already existing. The style sheet can be the one currently attached to the document, or it can be one attached to a document loaded into memory. When you insert a new style tag, *Microsoft Word* will automatically renumber all the style tags from that point to the end of the style sheet.

- Press the Esc key and type the letter G. This will display the style sheet currently attached to the document or division.

- If the style sheet is not currently attached to the text file, type the letters *TL* and press the F1 key. This will display the list of available style sheets.
- Use the arrow keys to move the highlight to your selection.
- Press the Enter key.
- Use the arrow keys to move the highlight to the position where you want to insert a new style tag.

- Type the letter *I*.
- Type in a two-letter code for the new style tag.
- Use the right-arrow key to move the highlight to Usage. Type the first letter of the type of style tag you're creating.
- Use the down-arrow key to move the highlight to Remark. In all capital letters, type in the remark you want to use to identify the function of the style tag. You are allowed up to 28 characters, including spaces.
- You can accept the variant suggested by *Microsoft Word*, or you can call the list and select another. If you want to change it, use the left arrow to move to it and then press the F1 key to call the list and make your selection. *Microsoft Word* will require you to authorize overwriting the existing variant setting.

252

- You can go back and change anything if it's incorrect. When ready to record the new style tag, press the Enter key.
- The new style tag will insert above the style tag marked with the cursor highlight. The style tags below that point will be renumbered automatically.

Formatting a new or existing style tag. The second part of creating a new style tag is to assign its formatting attributes. But this same process can be used to redefine any existing style tag in any style sheet. You can always go back and change the formatting instructions in a style tag.

Once you have the new tag inserted, it will be mostly empty of formatting instructions. You will assign the instructions to be used by using the Gallery Format menus. The steps below assume that you have just inserted a blank style tag with the steps in the preceding subsection and that you are still at the Gallery menu with the style sheet displayed.

- Make sure the highlight is on the style tag to be assigned format instructions.
- Type the letter *F* (Format).
- Now type the first letter of the kind of formatting you wish to assign to the style tag. This will call the respective menu.
- Set up the menu for the specific format attributes you wish to assign to the style tag.
- Press the Enter key.
- Repeat the steps above for any of the other types of format attributes.
- Save the style sheet.

As you assign the various attributes to the style tag, the information will be reflected in the onscreen display. Read it carefully, to make sure that it contains only the formatting attributes you want assigned to the style tag. You can always go back and make corrections.

Making a style tag from an existing tag. It's very simple to create a new style tag from an existing one. This is useful when the new tag is to vary only partially from the old one. The steps below presume that you already have a style sheet displayed at the Gallery menu.

Chapter 25

- Put the highlight on the style tag to be used as the pattern for the new one.

[C]
- Type C (Copy).
- Press the insert key. This will insert an exact duplicate of the old style tag.

- Rename the style tag. Give it a new remark that identifies it as being distinct from the tag used as a pattern. You can also change the usage and the variant.
- Now change the formatting attributes with the Gallery Format menus.
- Repeat the steps above for any other tags you wish to add to the style sheet with this procedure.
- When you have added all the tags you intend, save the style sheet.
- To escape at any time without changing the the style tag, press the Esc key.

Copying a style tag to another style sheet. It's very simple to copy any style tag to another place in the style sheet, but you can also copy it to another style sheet. You simply use standard cut-and-paste procedures. The steps below presume that you already know how to load a style sheet for viewing.

- Load the style sheet with the style tag you want to use in another style sheet.
- Use the arrow keys to put the highlight on the style tag to be copied.

[C]
- Type C (Copy). This will send a copy of the style tag to the scrap.
- Now load the style sheet where you need to copy the style tag.

- Put the highlight on the style tag below the point where you wish to insert the copied tag.
- Press the Enter key.
- Save the style sheet.

If you have a mouse, you may mark and copy more than one style tag at a time. Or you may mark an entire style sheet with Shift-F10, copy the entire style sheet to the other sheet, then delete the tags you don't want. You can achieve the same end by merging one style sheet into another.

Deleting a style tag from a style sheet. Here are the steps necessary to delete a tag from an existing style sheet:

- Put the highlight on the style tag to be deleted.
- Either type *D* or press the Del key.

Index

alignment 79
Alpha command 15
arrow keys 16
banner
  head, over multicolumn 105
  text, over multicolumn 105–6
Bold character tag 71
Border command 13
borders 139–50
  drawing 13
  printer capabilities and 140–41
boxes 144–46
Center Justification paragraph format 81
CGA graphics 4, 179
changed features, from previous versions 15–17
change tracking 13–14
character
  formatting, fast 72–73
  leader 121
characters, formatting 69–76
character style tag 237, 240
character tag 69
  bold 71
  double-hidden text 75–76
  double underline 71–72
  font sizes, and 74–75
  hidden text 75
  italic 71
  options 71–72
  small caps 72
  strikethrough 72
  subscript 74
  superscript 73–74
  underline 781
  uppercase 72
columns
  center-justified 124–25
  decimal 124
  left-justified 124
  right-justified 124
command
  Alpha, now not supported 15
  bar 9–10, 22, 23
  border 13
  card 25
  explanation, onscreen 18
  field. *See* command, bar
  menu 5, 21
  Transfer Merge 123

command area. *See* command, bar
commands
  choosing 17
  DOS 204
  Format 65–67
  Format Division 101
  Jump Page 47–49
  keyboard 5, 21–23
  Line-Draw 149
  mouse 21–23
  Transfer Glossary 42–45
copying text 56–59
  mouse and 57–58
  to glossary 58–59
  with delete 58
CTRL key 16
cut and paste 53–54
data transfer. *See* file manipulation
default settings, formats 66
default style sheet 101
deleted files, recovering 40–41
deleting files from disk 39–40
deleting text 59–62
dictionary 218, 221–22
different printer, selecting 153
disk, merge print text to 20
disk, printing to 162–63
display
  customizing 17–18
  enhanced 69
display modes 190–92
division, definition of 99
division-break options 107, 109–11
division mark 100
  inserting 106–7
division style tag 237, 240
.DOC filename extension 31
document retrieval 10–12
DOS commands 204
double-hidden text character tag 75–76
double underline character tag 71–72
draft mode printing 156
drafts, multiple 194
Edit menu. *See* command, bar
EGA graphics 4, 179
END key 16
enhancements, in 4.0 17–20
ESC key 9–10, 15
  keyboard commands and 5
fast-loading files 34
fast-text mode 15

257

file manipulation 33–45
files
   deleted, recovering 40–41
   deleting from disk 39–40
   fast-loading files 34
   loading 28–29, 33–35
   merging 41
   renaming 41–42
   rules for naming 30–31, 37–38
   saving 30, 35–38
First Line paragraph format 79, 81–82
font sizes, character tags and 74–75
footer 167–74
   different for odd and even pages 171–72
   divisions and 170
   indenting 170
   making room for 169
   page numbering and 110, 173–74
   positioning vertically 171
   speed-formatting 168–69
   stacking 169
   status 168
   status, displaying 168
   turning off 169–70
footnotes 47, 49–50
footnote window 205–7
format
   changing 65–66
   copying with mouse 92
   searching and replacing 185–86
   searching for 179–181
   division commands 101
   Division Layout menu 94, 111
   Style Sheet menu 238, 239
format commands 65–67
formatting 69–76
   paragraphs 77–97
form documents, printing 164
Full Justification paragraph format 81
function keys 16, 23
Gallery menu 238–39, 247–48
Genius video adapter 19
getting started 27–32
   floppy disk system and 27
   hard drive system and 27–28
global search 47, 175–81
global search and replace 183–88
glossary 42–45, 61
   copying text to 58–59
   printing 163–64
graphics
   CGA 4, 179
   display 3–4, 191
   EGA 4, 179
   interface 3
gutter margins 102

header 167–74
   inserting 167–68
   making room for 169
   page numbering and 110
   speed-formatting 168–69
   status 168
   turning off 169–70
headers, stacking 169
Hercules GN222 video adapter 19
Hewlett-Packard Laserjet printers 6–7, 70
hidden text
   character tag 75
   printing 156–57
   spell checker and 217
high-bit ASCII 140
home key 16
hyphenation 209–12
   automatic 211–12
   manual 209–10
   with Full Justification paragraph format 81
IBM VGA mode 19
indenting 17
   ALT commands and 84
   default 85
   mouse and 84–85
indents
   hanging 83–84
   stepped 84
index
   compiling 232
   double-hiding text and 232
index generation 229–33
inserting text 62–64
insertion marks 14
italic character tag 71
jargon 217
Jump mode 47–50
Jump Page commands 47–49
Keep Follow paragraph format 80, 89
Keep Together paragraph format 80, 90
keyboard, printing directly from 162
keyboard commands 5, 21–23
leader characters 121
left indent 79
Left Indent paragraph format 81, 82
Left Justification paragraph format 80
library features, on command bar 12
Library Index command 230
line-draw commands 149
line-drawing mode 147–48
line numbers 14–15
   printing in documents 111–14
line spacing 79
line styles 139–40
loading files, 28–29, 33–35

macros 10, 12, 236
Main menu. *See* command, bar
margins
 controlling 101–3
 gutter 102
markers, text 175–77
memory, expanding 195
memory, running out of in windows 195
menus, multiple levels of 10
merge print test, to disk 20
merging files 41
mouse 3, 5, 34
 advantages of 5–6
 commands 21–23
moving text 62–64
multicolumn 105–6
multiple-column pages 103–4
multiple copies, printing 155–56
multiple documents, working with 192–93
naming files, rules for 30–31, 37–38
new features with *Microsoft Word* 4.0 9–20
Norton Utilities 40
numbering, progressive 216
numbering text 213–16
onscreen formatting 3–4
outline mode 223, 224
outlining 19
page-break identification 18
page count, headers and footers and 168
page format
 changing in a division 99–100
 controls 100
 defaults 101
 divisions and 99–114
 numbering 109–10
page numbers, printing in document 108–10
page size, controlling 101–3
pagination 14–15, 47–49, 166
paper feed 160–62
paragraph borders, removing 143–44
paragraph boxes 141–42
paragraph format
 Center Justification 81
 First Line 79, 81–82
 Full Justification 81
 Hyphenation with Full Justification 81
 Keep Follow 80, 89
 Keep Together 80, 90
 Left Indent 81, 82
 Left Justification 80
 Right Indent 81, 82

Right Justification 80
Side by Side 80
Space After 80, 88
Space Before 80, 87–88
paragraph sets 93
paragraph style tag 237, 240
PGA graphics 4
printer
 different, selecting 153
 drivers, guidelines for selecting 153–54
 fonts 69–71
 Hewlett-Packard Laserjet 6–7, 70
 port 154–55
 support 6–7
printing 151–66
 an unsaved file 29–30
 Draft mode 156
 form documents, 164
 glossaries, 163–64
 multiple copies, 155–56
 page numbers in document 108–10
 queued 164–66
 range option 157–59
 side-by-side 96–97
 to disk 162–63
progressive numbering 216
Proof menu 219
proper nouns 217
queued printing 164–66
quitting *Microsoft Word* 32
repeat formatting 92–93
revision-Marks feature 13–14
right indent 79
Right Indent paragraph format 81, 82
Right Justification paragraph format 80
ruler line 116–17
saving files 30, 35–38
saving often, importance of 35
scrap 54–56, 60–61
 symbols in 56
search options 177–78
secondary windows, guidelines for 196
selected text, printing 157–59
shift key 16
Side-by-Side paragraph format 80
side-by-side printing 93, 103–6
small caps character tag 72
small pages, printing 103
Space After paragraph format 80, 88
Space Before paragraph format 80, 87–88
spacing 86–88
speed formatting, paragraphs and 90–92
spelling, checking 217–22

259

spelling checker 19
spreadsheet data, *Microsoft Word* and 12–13
status line 14
strikethrough character tag 72
style sheet 19, 235–55
   attaching to document 239, 243
   changing 243, 248
   concept of 235–26
   default 101
   side-by-side formatting and 94–95
style sheets, Microsoft, list of 241–43, 245–46
style tag 237
   by example 250–51
   new, recording 240–41
   new, writing 241
subscript character tag 74
summary sheet
   attached to document 10–12
   printing 157
superscript character tag 73–74
tab
   custom, speed-deleting 119
   custom, speed-setting 118
   settings, default, changing 117
   stop, clearing 118
   stop, setting 117–18
table 123–38
   different-sized fonts and 128–31
   editing and reorganizing 131–38
   removing column from 134
   typing as single paragraph 125
table of contents 19–20, 223–28
   formatting 227–28
   generating 226–27
   marking document for 224–26
tabs 115–21
   drawing lines with 146
   mouse and 119
   types of 120
tab stops, measuring 115–16
tagged lines 142–43

tagging text 243–45
tags, searching and replacing 186–88
template, function key 23
text
   clearing 38–39
   copying 56–59
   display mode 191–92
   file 22
   formatting, types of 65
thesaurus 19, 222
.TMP files 40
transfer
   glossary commands 42–45
   menu 33–45
   merge command 123
   options, windows and 202–3
underline character tag 781
uppercase character tag 72
utilities disk, *Microsoft Word* 12
Ventura Publisher 69
voltage spike 35
widows and orphans 88–90
   printing and 159–60
window
   closing 199
   footnote 205–7
   moving 199–200
   options, setting 200–202
   reference-note 190
   saving 203
   transfer options, windows and 202–3
windows
   multiple 189–207
   secondary, guidelines for 196
   splitting 196–99
   zooming 18, 189–90, 207
word counting 20
word-wrap 28
wraparound columns 94
WYSIWYG 3, 31, 65, 101. *See also* onscreen formatting
WYSIWYG monitors 4